THE SAUKIE INDIANS

O SYMBOL of a vanished race,
  With folded arms and thoughtful face,
Thou standest in thy lofty place,
  O'erlooking all the lands,
Where through the ages multiplied,
In forests deep, on prairies wide,
There lived and loved and fought and died
  Thy many tribes and bands.

The face of Nature scarce they changed,
Her children they, all unestranged,
Where'er they would they freely ranged
  And were well satisfied.
Across the sea the white men came
With wills of iron, hearts of flame,
To take possession in the name
  Of Kings beyond the tide.

The red men looked on with amaze,—
They would not, could not change their ways
Of living in a few brief days,
  And grudgingly gave place:
Though here and there heroic bands
Sought to retain their best loved lands,
Perforce they heeded the demands
  Of an all-conq'ring race.

Some remnants of the tribes remain
Both east and west, on hill and plain,—
In school, in shop, on farm they train
  To take an honored place
In their own land, the best of earth,
As citizens, where human worth
Shall count for more than rank or birth
  Or wealth or pride of race.

LORADO TAFT'S COLOSSAL INDIAN STATUE AT OREGON, ILLINOIS *a*

THE SAUKIE INDIANS
And Their Great Chiefs
BLACK HAWK AND KEOKUK

By

AMER MILLS STOCKING, *1858-*

Samp-we-te-oh

(He who deals fairly)

A Descendant of the Wampanoags

With an Introduction by

ALICE FRENCH

(Octave Thanet)

ROCK ISLAND, ILLINOIS

THE VAILE COMPANY

1926

Printed in U.S.A.

To

MR. AND MRS. JOHN H. HAUBERG,

whose interest in the Historic
Past is exceeded only by their help-
fulness in the Living Present and
their hope for the Glorious Future.

PREFACE

THE North American Indians were the most unique and inscrutable of all peoples. For many centuries they occupied our land without molestation. It was their land then, and they yielded it unwillingly to the white invaders. Their heritage has become our heritage. That fact alone gives them claim to our notice. But they are interesting in themselves. Their racial peculiarities, their manners and customs, their legends and traditions and their known history are of the most absorbing interest.

The Sauks and Foxes for many years occupied the Central Mississippi valley, from the mouth of the Wisconsin to the mouth of the Missouri, and from the Illinois to western Iowa. Illinois, Wisconsin and Iowa are rich with the memory of them.

They were typical Indians, and they produced two of the greatest men of their race: Black Hawk, the great-souled patriot, whose love for his native village amounted to an obsession and who, in the face of the strongest opposition and discouragement, led the last vain effort put forth in the old Northwest to withstand the on-coming white men; and the far-sighted Keokuk, no less patriotic, who chose the pathway of peace and friendship.

There is not wanting literature regarding the Sauks and Foxes. Schoolcraft, Atwater, Catlin and others have written about them, there are several histories of the Black Hawk War, and a number of biographies of Black Hawk, including the remarkable and intensely interesting book dictated by himself.

The present work has been undertaken and carried on with five controlling purposes:

Careful investigation;
Attractive presentation;
A fair degree of completeness;
The greatest possible accuracy;
Absolute impartiality.

In the early chapters a background of primitive conditions is given; and throughout an effort has been made to connect the history with the larger history of the United States, which should make the book especially suitable for supplementary reading in high schools.

The writing is in standard verse. The style, however, is plain and straightforward, with little effort at poetic adornment. The meter is frequently changed, so that reading is not likely to become wearisome. It may be that some "kind readers" or some kind of readers will find this story of the Saukies more vivid and interesting because of the style of composition.

Grateful acknowledgments are made:

To Mr. and Mrs. John H. Hauberg for kindly encouragement, and the privilege of making selections from their fine collection of Indian pictures for use as Illustrations;

To Miss Alice French (Octave Thanet) for valuable suggestions and the much prized Introduction;

To Mr. Ben H. Wilson for assistance in investigations, the preparation of the maps and the securing of photographs;

To Mrs. Jessie Palmer Webber, Secretary of the State Historical Society of Illinois, and Mr. Benjamin F. Shambaugh, Superintendent of the State Historical Society of Iowa, for the courtesies of their offices;

To Professor Francis G. Blair for reading the manuscript;

To Reverend R. G. Smith, Mr. Joseph Svancina, Miss Grace R. Meeker, Miss Mary Jayne, Mrs. John Earl Keokuk, Mr. H. M. Anschutz, Mr. Frank E. Stevens, Mr. Lorado Taft, Col. D. M. King and others for kindly assistance.

Specific credit will be given in the notes for the use of material for illustrations.

AMER MILLS STOCKING.

Peoria, Illinois, 1926.

ILLUSTRATIONS AND MAPS

CONTENTS

xi

Contents

INTRODUCTION

AN enormous amount of serious study and first-hand research is concealed beneath this unassuming metrical epic of the Saukies and the Foxes.

Its form, with the rippling meter and the rhymed ballads, seems at first blush to deny any real historical labor, or long continued critical investigation; but a very little reading discloses not only the entire spontaneity of the form with the writer but the thoroughness of his preparation.

Between the covers here there is more than the record of a fast fading era in our mid-western history, valuable as the record is. There are keys to historical puzzles never adequately solved; there is a light held up over some of our time blurred mistakes in dealing with the red man; and everywhere we have sympathetic, keen portraits of Indians.

Here is the real, human Black Hawk, versatile, eloquent, daring, impetuous, shrewd in a large way, ruthless occasionally but magnanimous and with a pathetic love for his land and his people, a ruler of vision yet again simple as a child. Take for instance his naive comment on the Negro and offer to take over any slave surplus in "helping the women do the work."*

Here, also, we have the wise old Keokuk, one of our greatest Indians, the wily Poweshiek, the faithful Appanoose and a multitude of forgotten warriors and frontier leaders who did not deserve the oblivion which has gathered over their fame.

We can put a truer value on that little Black Hawk War. If a little war it had large issues. And some of our mightiest figures moved through this almost forgotten warfare which blundered to a conclusion through more defeats than victories. Andrew Jackson was president those days; Winfield Scott was commander in chief; one of the regular officers was a brilliant and most efficient young Southerner,

---

*Quoted in the notes, which are uncommonly interesting.

Jefferson Davis; and the Captain of one of the militia companies (who studied the drill book at night and practiced it by day, not always with good fortune) was a long, lean, awkward small town lawyer of the Northwest, Abraham Lincoln.

Not only the rulers of men walk across these pages,—they need no one's introduction to youth, although it is good to catch intimate glimpses of them before they were famous; unknown but not unhelpful heroes walk and fight and crisp our spines. The writer brushes the dust of oblivion off many a fine deed. Again the sturdy frontiersmen make us proud of their courage, their fortitude, their versatile ingenuity. Again Street shows that an Indian Agent may be honest and wise in a large way and do vastly important things for his country and his wards without reward. Again Dodge makes his dogged fight against bureaucratic arrogance and stupidity. And there is a glimpse of honest, kindly wise old Antoine LeClaire.

Not the leaders only get belated praise or blame. There is the pathetic story of the preacher, Adam Payne, so devoted to his faith, so simple and so cruelly murdered. There is the ballad of the peerless horseman (he bore the amazing name of Ziba Dimmick—was ever a hero more mishandled in nomenclature!) who whistled through the chinks of the beleaguered log cabin to his pet pony; and when he answered, made a dash for his back, mounted, rode through a storm of Indian bullets; and with neither saddle or bridle threaded the pathless forest and reached Hennepin twenty miles away, in time to rally aid and drive off the savages. The book is crowded with the like samples of the stuff which won the prairies; deeds of daring-do warranted to send a thrill down any true American spine.

The dust of the busy travel of generations has gathered over these spacious, heroic days. Yet they are worth remembering. The mistakes which their ignorance, their callous greed and blind prejudices of race or creed made; we make to-day in other forms to other people. They paid for them.

For some of them we are still paying to-day. It is well to study them and take warning. Their rugged virtues we need.

Whoever shall renew their time and make them live again deserves well of his country. Therefore, Dr. Stocking, I thank you, I wish you a multitude of readers; and I feel that because of their reading they will become better and wiser and truer Americans.

OCTAVE THANET.

THE SAUKIE INDIANS

And Their Great Chiefs

BLACK HAWK AND KEOKUK

I. THE UNDISCOVERED LAND

THROUGHOUT the long ages a continent lay
Decked out by Dame Nature in virgin array
Of mountain and valley, of forest and plain,
Of lake and of stream flowing down to the main.
From great sea to great sea the vast region was rife
With the full and free play of all animal life,
From the sweet-singing bird to the king of the air,
From the beaver and mink to the bison and bear.

Save far to the south where the Aztec held sway
And wrought with great skill till the close of his day,
Scarce a trace could be seen of the thought and the plan
And the physical labor of civilized man:
No cities uprearing their towers and spires,
No furnaces belching the flames of their fires,
No farm-houses dotting the valley and plain,
No great fields awave with the ripening grain,
No roadways of steel where the trains come and go,
No shafts deeply sunk to the rich ores below.

Great earth-mounds there were that to this day remain
In some parts of the land on the hilltop and plain:
They were made by hard toil in the years long ago,
But even their purpose we scarcely may know.
And the builders themselves, did they yield up their place
To others who came as a conquering race,

1

Or did their descendants by changing their ways
Become the wild tribes of the more recent days?
These things we would know will remain all untold
Till the great scroll of time shall at last be unrolled.

But wild people there were who for uncounted years
Lived out their wild lives with their hopes and their fears,
With their loves and their hates, with their pleasures and
    pains,
With whatever they deemed to be losses or gains.
They were scattered abroad in their tribes and their bands
Through the forests and plains of the far-reaching lands.

Their dwellings were wigwams or booths or tepees.
Consisting of poles or the branches of trees,
With bark or with mats or with skins covered o'er,
A flap at one side being left for a door,
While within all around mats and skins were outspread
To serve double purpose of seat and of bed.
A space in the center was left for a fire
And a hole in the top for the smoke to aspire.

Their food was the flesh of the game that they slew
With the spear or the club or the arrow that flew
Straight on to its mark with a low whizzing song
From the bow-string drawn back by the hand quick and
    strong;
Or perchance that was caught in the dead-fall or snare
That had been well prepared and was set with great care.
Sometimes they had also the corn and the beans
And the pumpkins or squashes produced by the means
Of the women's painstaking and arduous toil,
As with sticks, stones and bones they dug into the soil.
Sometimes as a food roots and barks were employed,
Nuts and fruits in their season were greatly enjoyed,
And a syrup was made that was fit for a king,
From the sap of the maple that flowed in the spring.

Like all savage tribes they were scantily clad,
Not that garments made roughly they might not have had,
But because they considered all clothing to be
In restraint of their movements, and wished to be free;
So a strip of soft skin round the loins was made fast
And as needed a skin o'er the shoulder was cast.
The body and limbs that were left so exposed
Were treated with oil as their state well disclosed.

Their wigwams and all of their personal gear
For a personal use were possessed without fear
Of question or loss, but well they gave heed
To the general good, to the primary need;
And the poorest and weakest of those in a band
Lacked not food and clothing when these were at hand.
It was no easy task to make store of supplies,
And indeed in such things they were not always wise,
For freely they used what they had to the last,
And a feast oftentimes yielded place to a fast.

There was much of affection in family life,
And though all the drudging devolved on the wife,
While the husband as hunter and warrior beplumed
Roamed about, all this drudging was freely assumed.
Such a thing was unknown as employment for hire,
And even a Chieftain who chanced to aspire
An establishment fitting his rank to maintain,
As a means to accomplish his purpose was fain,
Not fearful of serious family strife,
To take on now and then an additional wife.
In neighborly touch there was little constraint,
Yet seldom indeed was there cause for complaint;
But if quarrels arose there was one rule forsooth,
"An eye for an eye and a tooth for a tooth."
(Though two eyes for an eye and two teeth for a tooth
They greatly preferred, and again a "forsooth.")
If a murder was done, neither fire nor flood

Could hold back very long the avenger of blood;
Though sometimes in spite of resentment and pride
Gifts were taken and thus tears of sorrow were dried.

They lived a half settled, half wandering life,
Forever with beasts and each other at strife,
With a summer home here and a hunting ground there
And frequent excursions almost anywhere.
In a general way each tribe had a claim
To a district or region for dwellings and game;
But boundary lines were not drawn hard and fast,
And possessory right was known only to last
As long as the occupants' powers in fight
Were sufficient to prove that they had such a right.
If too weak to oppose a more powerful foe
They went forth in their turn other tribes to o'erthrow,
Or to find some unoccupied place in the land
Where unhunted they might for a time take their stand.

Their glory and pride was in what is called war,
With no more and no less of a reason therefor
Than has moved other men throughout the long years
And bathed every country in blood and in tears.

Each tribe held the fiction that they were the men,
The strong and the brave and the righteous, and when
Other men stood against them they always were wrong
And must be perforce brought to sing their death song.
Their method of carrying forward their strife
Was in fullest accord with their method of life:
The lessons they learned from the wild beasts of prey
And in hunting made use of, were brought into play
As they went to contend with their own savage kind,
With the hope of a victory always in mind.
They cared not in large numbers to meet hand to hand,
But the ambush and raid were most carefully planned,
The stealthy approach and the blood-curdling cry,

The attack on the weak when no helper was nigh.
They always endeavored advantage to take
And the utmost of every advantage to make.

Unbelievably cruel when they overcame
They joined in an orgy of blood and of flame.
From immediate death certain ones they would spare
To take to their village and execute there,
With tortures more dreadful than one in our time
Would dare try to describe or in prose or in rhyme.
The victim who might have been victor instead,
Went forth to his doom with a resolute tread;
To his enemies round he hurled back taunt for taunt,
And raising his death song continued to vaunt
Himself and his tribe, and their cause to defend
Till death brought the terrible scene to an end.

Sometimes among this most inscrutable race
One chosen for torture was given the place
Of a brother or son, who in war had been slain,
And continued through life such a place to maintain.
More often a girl taken captive was reared
To be wife of the brave that most greatly she feared.

So they lived out their lives, undoubtedly free
As the beasts and their passions allowed them to be,
But with no thought of progress, no wish to aspire
To things that were nobler and broader and higher,
With no call from without and no stir from within,
Content to remain as their fathers had been.

Thus in wild isolation the continent lay,
Till the hand of Columbus the veil drew away,
And the Old World, beholding the long-hidden prize,
Was aroused to adventure and high enterprise.

II. THE WHITE MAN'S TOUCH

IT was early determined each nation should hold
  That part of the land its discoverers bold
Should be first to claim in the name of their king,
And the proofs of priority clearly could bring.

To the rights of the natives they gave little thought,
But rather to teach them their own ways they sought.
The Indians were ready for friendship and trade,
But preferred their own path to that white men had made:
The things that helped out in their own way of life
They were glad to obtain, from a pot to a knife;
But from any suggestion of progress by toil,
Howe'er it was made, they were quick to recoil.
They accepted the hoe, but rejected the plow,
Made use of the horse, but cared not for the cow;
They seized on the hatchet, but hated the ax;
They traded for blankets, but would not raise flax;
They were eager for guns and for water of fire,
But for civilized life they had little desire.

The proud Spaniards came to coerce and subdue,
But they purposed to teach and evangelize too.
The island inhabitants melted away
Before them like dew in the heat of the day;
And the Aztecs were forced in their evil hour
To yield up their all to this conquering power.

HATUEY, THE REBELLIOUS SLAVE[1]

From Hayti, 'neath the Spanish heel,[2]
  A Chieftain with his band
Sought native freedom to regain
  On Cuba's fairer strand.

6

The months had barely stretched to years
   When Spanish boats appeared;
And all the things from which they'd fled
   Again they sadly feared.

The Chieftain said: "The Spanish god
   We must propitiate.
Behold him!   Let us ask this gold
   To save from cruel fate."

But then he said: "No, no, this god
   Is theirs, and will betray
Us to his special devotees,—
   We must throw him away."

The Spaniards came: they caught the Chief
   And quickly orders gave,
That he should perish at the stake
   As a rebellious slave.

They bound him fast and gathered wood;
   But ere they kindled fire,
With hope to save his precious soul,
   There came a zealous friar.

"Permit me," said the holy man,
   "In God's name to baptize,
Then you will pass from horrid death
   To joys of paradise."

The Chieftain said: "Are Spaniards there?
   That first I would enquire."
"There are, but only those who're good,"
   Returned the worthy friar.

"The best of them are nothing worth,"
　　The doomed man made reply.
"I want no chance of meeting them:
　　Leave me in peace to die."

The French in the north with their kindlier ways,
Made friendships that lasted for many long days.
Their own dispositions, the trend of their lives,
Their aptness to take to them Indian wives,
The climate, the fur trade, the land rough and wide,
Made easy their dwelling in peace side by side.

But their Indian allies had their Indian foes,
And the Frenchmen with these must perforce come to blows:
From Quebec on the east to the far Illinois
They fought many times with the brave Iroquois.
With the Foxes and others they also had strife,
And were never immune from the dread scalping knife.

CHAMPLAIN'S WAR EXPEDITION WITH THE ALGONQUINS [3]

Champlain from the time of his coming
　　In the year sixteen hundred and three
Sustained with the native Algonquins
　　Relations as fair as could be.

He founded Quebec and established
　　With the Indians a lucrative trade,
While at all times, carefully, efforts
　　Conducive to friendship were made.

The Indians desired his assistance
　　In war 'gainst their Iroquois foe;
And wishing to make explorations,
　　He gladly consented to go.

There were three white men in the party,
    All seeking fresh glory to gain:
They ascended the Richelieu river
    To the beautiful Lake Champlain.

Soon after they met with the foemen,
    Who said they were willing to fight;
But as it was late in the evening,
    They camped side by side through the night.

They kept up a constant reviling,
    And with the first dawn of the day
Their savage forces were marshaled
    In opposing battle array.

The advancing Algonquins divided
    By plan preconcerted, and thus
To Champlain the best chance was given
    For discharging his great arquebus.[4]

Two Chieftains fell dead, and a warrior
    Badly wounded was laid at their side:
The Iroquois trembled with wonder,
    Not knowing what next might betide.

They shot a few scattering arrows,
    Determined to keep up the fight;
But another gun roared from the forest,
    And they turned in precipitate flight.

The Algonquins pursuing killed others
    And captured a dozen or more:
Returning they gathered the booty
    And danced with great joy on the shore.

After traveling homeward some distance
    They halted to torture a brave:
They reviled him and forced him to singing,
    But sad was the song that he gave.

Champlain tells the tale of the torture
    In all of its frightful detail,
From the horrible deeds of the captors
    To the pain-crazy prisoner's wail.

They asked him to join in the torture;
    But he told them the man should be slain
At once. To this they objected
    Saying: "Then he would suffer no pain."

He turned from their presence heart-sickened.
    Not wishing to gain his ill will,
They told him he might take his musket
    And shoot out the ball that would kill.

Not satisfied then, the dead body
    They mangled and cut as they chose,
That to the last end the mere matter
    Might feel the dread hatred of foes.

So they journeyed on to the parting:
    Each band took its prisoners then,
And with great protestations of friendship
    Bade farewell to the mighty white men.

They asked them to always be brothers,
    And help them whenever they could.
Champlain, who valued their friendship,
    Replied that they certainly would.

For the first time near the Atlantic
    Whites had fought as Indian allies;
And the first time in these northern regions
    Fire arms had been used in this wise.

Beyond that it started a blood-feud
    'Twixt the Iroquois tribes and the French,
That continued till both the contenders
    Were stripped of all power at length.

To the English the heart of the continent fell,
And the lovers of liberty came here to dwell.
To make homes for themselves they were chiefly intent
And to the set task all their powers they bent.

With the Indians peaceful relations they sought,
They treatied and trafficked and traded and bought:
Not always was full and just recompense made,
Opportunists they were and they liked a good trade.
Sometimes there were dif'rences, discord and strife,
And terrible warfare with sad loss of life.
Whatever the losses that each side sustained,
In the end it was found that the colonists gained.

OPECHANCANOUGH'S CHALLENGE

The Emperor-Chief, Powhatan,
   In honor and age passed away;
Opitchipan Chieftain became,—
   Opechancanough really had sway.[5]

By them the old leagues were confirmed,
   And new vows of friendship were made;
When confidence fully was won
   The Indians uplifted the blade.

The year was sixteen twenty-two,
   And March twenty-second the day;
Throughout all Virginia the reds
   Arose and proceeded to slay.

The blows were all struck at one time:
   Three hundred and forty and seven
White corpses were laid in their gore,
   'Neath the pitying eye of fair heaven.

Then followed a long, bloody war,
   The issue was white men or red:
It was settled when many of both
   Had been sent to the ranks of the dead.

MASSASOIT AND KING PHILIP

The great Chief, Massasoit,
  Sent Samoset to greet
The Plymouth colonists,
  And came himself to treat[6]
With them as new inhabitants,
Who in his country sought a chance
  To make their lives complete.

The treaty that day made,
  In spite of doubts and fears,
Preserved a helpful peace
  For well nigh fifty years.
They lived as friendly people should
And ever sought each other's good,
  At least it so appears.

But dif'rences arose,—
  King Philip came to power,
He thought the whites unjust
  And for them would not cower.
He gathered all the Indian bands
To drive the white men from the lands:
  It was his day and hour.

The sea of bloody war
  In wildest waves was tossed.
The toll of white men's lives
  Was fearful in its cost.
Death claimed two thousand Indian braves,
And many more were sold as slaves:
  The natives' cause was lost.

III. THE MIGRATIONS OF THE SAUKS
AND FOXES

THE Sauks were Algonquins who occupied lands
Near where the great city of Montreal stands.
Traditions prevail that Chief Nanamakee
First welcomed Champlain when he came o'er the sea,
That between them a compact of friendship was made
And for a long time they continued to trade.

So far as is known there was nothing to quench
The fires of true friendship 'twixt Saukies and French;
But the Sauks were a warlike and quarrelsome band,[7]
And other tribes joined to drive them from the land.[8]

They sojourned in Michigan near a great bay,
That their modified name carries down to this day.[9]
Then they went up to Mackinac, thence o'er the lake
In hopes there a permanent village to make.
Having built at Green Bay, they began to gain strength
And made with the Foxes a treaty at length.

THE CAPTURE OF FORT MACKINAC[10]

Mechillimackinac,
    There's music in the name:
It sings of woods and lakes,
    Adventure, love and fame.

From out its ample store
    One incident we bring,
One story that shall last
    While time is on the wing.

It was on June the fourth
    Of seventeen sixty-three;

The English at the fort
    Were in authority.

The Chippewas and Sauks
    Had volunteered to play,
In honor of the King,
    The game, baggatiway.

Far distant posts were set
    The goals to designate;
The center of the field
    Was near the fortress gate.

The squaws of both the tribes
    Were seated on the ground,
In solemn quietness
    With blankets wrapped around.

The soldier at their ease
    Were witnessing the game;
The gate was open wide,
    And no one seemed to blame.

Each player bore a rod
    With hoop-net at the end,
With which to lift the ball
    And carry it, or send

It hurtling through the air
    Toward the goal he sought:
The interest in the game
    To highest pitch was wrought.

Here stood the Chippewas,
    And there the mighty Sauks;
The wagers then were laid
    For always "money talks."

The umpire threw the ball
　Between them on the ground;
The naked Indians
　Sprang forward with a bound.

Here, there and everywhere
　Their agile forms are seen;
They flash beneath the sun,
　The bronze above the green.

Sometimes they close in groups,
　Each seeking for the ball;
One scoops it in his net,
　Then quick apart they fall.

The lucky player tries
　To carry without loss
While each opponent seeks
　To strike it from his crosse.

If pressed too close by foes
　The runner seeks to send,
By quick and dextrous toss
　The ball toward a friend.

Or if he finds a place
　In which to make a swing,
He speeds it on its way
　With one tremendous fling.

Excitement grows intense:
　Mid shouts and wild hurrahs,
Now Saukies make a gain
　And now the Chippewas,

When suddenly the ball,
　Not by mischance or fate,

But cleverest design,
   Is thrown within the gate.

The players with a yell
   Rush forward, and the squaws
Rise up and give them arms,
   These Sauks and Chippewas.

No longer peaceful men,
   Who play baggatiway
And help to celebrate
   The British King's birthday;

They were at once transformed,
   As through the gate they went
To howling savages
   On massacre intent.

No need to here record
   What followed in detail:
The Indians took the fort,
   And we let down the veil.

THE FOXES AND THE FRENCH

The Musquawkies were also Algonquins
   Early known to the white men from France,
Who called them *Les Reynards* or Foxes
   And looked on them always always askance.

For this reason or for some other
   They followed the Iroquois lead
And made it quite plain to the Frenchmen
   That they were *Les Reynards* indeed.

The result was that they were persuaded,
   By force or by urgent request,
To leave the Canadian country
   And seek for a home farther west.

In the war 'twixt the French and the English
    That came in the time of Queen Anne,
The Iroquois, pledged to be neutral,
    Their allies drew into a plan

To put down the Frenchmen forever.
    The Foxes, alert and adroit,
Soon gathered, two thousand in number,
    Before the French fort at Detroit.

Du Boisson, commanding, had thirty
    Brave traders and *coureur du bois,*
These only to act as defenders
    'Gainst the friends of the dread Iroquois.

His weakness was also apparent
    In a very small store of supplies.
He succeeded in sending out runners
    To summon his Indian allies.

Pottawatomies, Ottawas, Hurons
    Responded, but they were afraid
To make an assault on the Foxes,
    Behind a well built barricade.

Under siege for long days the brave Foxes
    Were dying of hunger and thirst;
But their bowstrings still sent flaming arrows
    To the fort.   They were doing their worst.

The allies became very impatient,
    They longed to engage in a fight;
And so at the last they determined
    To make an assault in the night.

They scaled the rude wall and sprang downward
    With a whoop that might startle the dead;
But they found the encampment deserted,
    For the Foxes had quietly fled.

The next day the allies overtook them,
    And slew a large number of braves;
A few were reserved for the torture,
    And the women were spared to be slaves.

Unsubdued were the Foxes remaining,
    And crazed to avenge their hard fate,
They lurked at each ford and each portage,
    For their enemies lying in wait.

As the fire-brands of the country
    They were everywhere hated and feared,
And seemed doomed to utter destruction
    Till the Sauks as a savior appeared.

We are told by Black Hawk that each nation
    Was too weak to contend with its foes.
From their mutual need of assistance
    A treaty of friendship arose.

It was made at Green Bay in a council
    And was faithfully kept through the years:
Not a hint of dissatisfaction
    On any known record appears.

A Seventeenth Century Incident

Near Montreal, in early days,
The Foxes and the Chippewas
    In warfare found employ.
The wily Foxes shrewdly made
Upon the Chippewas a raid
    And carried off a boy.

The lad was Ojawatama,
The son of mighty Bianswa,
    A Chief well known to fame,
Who from the village was away

Upon that most momentous day
  The crafty Foxes came.

When he returned, this warrior bold,
Those at the village quickly told
  The most heart-rending tale.
He bade farewell to kindred dear,
Then without tomahawk or spear,
  He struck the Foxes trail.

He traveled fast and traveled long
And reached their village as a throng
  Of Foxes surged around,
While some prepared a fire to make
Of faggots scattered near a stake
  To which his boy was bound.

They had not yet begun their dance
When Bianswa made his advance
  As quickly as he could.
Proceeding with a manly stride,
In all his royal strength and pride
  He in the circle stood,

And to the wondering Foxes said:
"I come to give myself instead
  Of my son at the stake,
To ask that you will set him free,
And that in place of him, on me
  You will your vengeance take.

"He has not many winters seen,
The leaves upon his tree are green,
  He's not with you at strife.
His feet have never trod the path
Of war, he merits not your wrath.
  Will you not spare his life?"

"My hairs are whitened by the frost,
My strength and force are almost lost,
　　Although my heart is brave.
I've had my share of joy and grief,
My tree now bears the yellow leaf,
　　I'm ready for the grave.

"Full many scalps from off your braves
These hands have hung above the graves
　　Of my own tribe and kin.
Upon me wreck your vengeance dire,
About me you should kindle fire.
　　At once your work begin."

To this the Foxes gave consent,
And with their cries the heavens rent.
　　Away the boy was led,
And firmly to the victim's stake,
That they on him might vengeance take,
　　The Chief was bound instead.

They tortured him with all their skill,
But could not break his stubborn will,
　　Or bring from him a groan.
Thus did great Bianswa expire,
Thus for another take the fire
　　Upon himself alone.

FORT ARMSTRONG, DAVENPORT, ROCK ISLAND AND MOLINE IN 1844
From painting by J. C. Wild

b

IV. THE SEIZURE OF THE ROCK
ISLAND COUNTRY

THE Sauk and Fox Indians were long at Green Bay,
The Sauk and Fox rivers still speak of their stay;
While on the Wisconsin their footprints are seen
At Prairie du Sac and Prairie du Chien.[11]

Their young men, adventurous, roamed far and wide
With their Indian sense as a trustworthy guide;
And ever, returning, they told of a land,
Where the tall forest trees by the great rivers stand,
While broad prairies, covered with rich verdure, lie
Stretched out in their beauty conveniently by,
A land of rich fruitage, of game and of fish,
A land that was all that an Indian might wish.

The hearts of the Sauks and the Foxes were fired,
And a home in that eden they greatly desired.
They gathered their forces, and with one consent
With all they possessed down the Rock River went.
Arriving, they drove the Kaskaskias away,
Took the land for their own, and determined to stay
As long as the trees of the forest should grow,
The flowers should bloom and the great waters flow.

No fairer land beneath the sun
Has through the years been lost and won,
Than where Rock River's flashing tide
Speeds on to meet the waters wide,
The mighty Mississippi sends
Down to the gulf and earth's far ends.

The Santeaux, who were Chippewas,
Held all that land in early days,
But later on, the French have told,

21

'Twas taken by the warriors bold,
Who called themselves the Kickapoos.
Their fate it was in turn to lose
To brave Kaskaskias, known to fame,
Who held it when the Saukies came.[12]

"THE CAVE OF DEATH"—"THE MAIDEN'S BOWER"

Long, long before the Saukies
  Obtained the valley lands,
The Watch Tower and the country round
  Were in the Santeaux' hands.

Their young and mighty War Chief
  Was greatly loved and feared:
One day the village learned with grief
  That he had disappeared.

The Peace Chiefs sent the crier
  To call the people in,
That they might plan a careful search
  And soon the work begin.

Some, passing up the river,
  Stopped at the big spring cave:
The sight they saw congealed their blood,
  Although their hearts were brave.

Beneath the rock o'erhanging,
  The Chief's dead body lay;
His heart was on his naked breast,
  His scalp-lock torn away.

His skull was crushed, its contents
  Were scattered here and there;
His open eyes were turned above,
  In fixed and glassy stare.

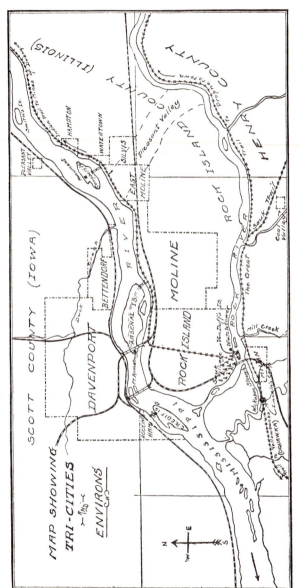

Map of the Three City Region
Drawn by Ben H. Wilson

The party gave the signal,
    The tale of horror spread,
And sadly all the Santeaux came
    To look upon the dead.

No sign was found of warriors
    From any hostile band:
They felt the Manitou had done
    The deed with his own hand.

Perhaps the Chief was guilty
    Of crimes to them unknown
And so this fearful punishment
    Was wrought on him alone.

The place from that day forward
    Was shunned by all the tribe,
As full of horror and of dread,
    That no one could describe.

            .   .   .   .   .

The years passed on, and Dove Eye,
    The Head Man's daughter fair,
Although full well the tale she knew,
    Alone went often there.

She mused beside the fountain,
    Or bent with easy grace
Above the ever placid pool,
    That mirrored back her face.

It was her dressing chamber:
    Safe from intrusion there,
She laved her dusky Indian form
    And decked her raven hair.

And so the big spring grotto,
    Beyond the great Watch Tower,

That long was called "The Cave of Death,"
Became "The Maiden's Bower."

The Saukies constructed their principal town
At the foot of the bluff where The Tower slopes down,
By the rapid Rock River, three miles from its mouth,
And from the Great River as far to the South.
The Foxes crossed into the Iowa lands
And made their chief village where Davenport stands.[13]

They extended their sway far east and far south
To the Illinois River and down to its mouth.
They laid covetous eyes on the lands to the west,
And, proving their powers of warfare were best,
They made the less militant Iowas yield
A large part of these lands for a great hunting field,
Down to the DesMoines, and even below,
Where through the deep forests the Two Rivers flow.

But they were not deprived of the Indian's delight,
A foeman both able and willing to fight:
When they wished, they could meet with a Cherokee
    band,
Or some other tribe that was nearer at hand,
While they always had all that they might wish to do,
In holding their own with the terrible Sioux.

V. THE YEARLY ROUND OF SAUKIE LIFE

As Portrayed by Black Hawk

DESCRIPTION OF THE COUNTRY

FOR more than a century we had possessed[14]
That part of the country, the finest and best,
That the Father of Waters so grandly flows through
From Wisconsin's fair stream to the Portage des Sioux.[15]

On the bank of Rock River the Sauk village stood:
Below was the prairie, above was the wood
Adorning the hillside with many a bower,
And crowning the height of the beautiful tower,
From whence there were prospects outspread in all ways
To allure and reward every visitor's gaze.

On the side of the Bluff stretching out to the north
For two miles, were the fields of most excellent worth,
Which became, through the toil of our women, the means
Of supplying us all with corn, squashes and beans.
The springs gave us drink that was all we could wish,
And the Rock River rapids afforded fine fish.
With hunger our children were ne'er known to cry
We always had plenty our wants to supply.

Not far from the village our grave-yard was spread,
Our own Chip-pi-an-nock, the home of our dead;
Where the mother could weep oe'r the grave of her child
And think of its nature, so gentle and mild;
And the warrior, returning with victory's boast,
At the tomb of his sire could again paint the post.
There is no place like this to repair to in grief:
Here indeed the Great Spirit will bring us relief.

The Return to the Village from the Winter Hunt

When we come to our village again in the spring
From our wintering grounds, finest peltries we bring
And continue to barter with traders who come
Bringing with them their goods, and a few kegs of rum,
That they usually promise to us in the fall,
If we make a good hunt, and are peaceful withal.
The bartering over, they leave us again
And then in a frolic join all our old men.

The next thing we do is to bury our dead,
Who during the year to Sowana have fled.
We count this to be a great medicine feast,
And the nearest of kin to those who are deceased
Give away of their goods to each neighbor and friend,
Until they have nothing on which to depend,
In hopes the Great Spirit himself will engage
To pity their lot and their grief to assuage.

Then we open our caches and take from them all
The provisions we put there the previous fall,
Repair all our lodges and fences and clear
Up the cornfields for planting the crop of the year.
This work by the women is done, while the men
The events of the winter are telling again,
And feasting on wild fowl and dried meats, and maize
Prepared with great care in a number of ways.

The Crane Dance, Courting and Marriage

When the corn has been planted, there's feasting always,
And we dance the Crane dance for two or three days.
Our women dance with us in gaudy attire,
And then for the young men, who have the desire
To marry, the proper occasion arrives
For selecting the maidens they wish to make wives.

Each man tells his mother the choice he has made,
For she in the project must be his chief aid.
She confers with the chosen one's mother, and then
The time for a call is appointed, and when
It arrives he proceeds to the lodge in the night,
Awakens his loved one and making a light
Holds it close to her face and then close to his own,
That each to the other may be fully known.
If she blows out the light the transaction is done,
And next morning he wakes in the lodge as a son.
If, however, the light is permitted to burn,
To his own lodge the young man must quickly return.

The next day he comes back and stands boldly in view,
Playing softly his flute for his lady-love true.
The maids of the wigwam come out one by one
To discover, perhaps, for whom playing is done;
But the tune is soon changed, whosoe'er may appear,
Excepting the one whom his heart holds so dear.
When she comes to hear, he continues to play
His courting tune for her till she goes away.
He then ceases playing and waits till the night,
When a new trial usually turns out all right.

The first year they find if they well can agree
And be happy together as people should be.
If instead of contentment there's quarrel and strife,
They part and seek other companions for life.
If we lived on together with discord to mar
Our joys, we'd be foolish as white people are.

There is no indiscretion can banish a squaw
From the home of her parents by our social law.
No matter how many the children she brings,
The pot's on the fire, their welcome it sings.

THE WAR DANCE

Ere excitement attending the Crane dance has ceased
We begin to prepare for another great feast
And our national dance at which warriors are made,
That in face of our foes we may not be dismayed.

The great square in the village is swept and made clean,
The the Chiefs and old warriors appear on the scene:
They are seated on mats at the head of the square;
The drummers and singers are next to them there;
The women and braves at the sides take their place,
While the center is left as a broad open space.

The singing commences, the drums beats resound,
And a warrior springs into the space with a bound.
Keeping time to the music he plays well his part,
Showing how from the village the war parties start,
How then with great stealth he approaches the foe,
Leaps forth to his side, strikes him down with a blow,
Making use of the knife tears the scalp from his head,
And goes away leaving him bleeding and dead.
All join in applause and he then leaves the square,
And another one enters to take his place there.[16]

Such young men as ne'er have seen warfare and slain
An enemy, outside the square must remain
Each one stands aside at this time in his place,
While expressions of shame are beheld on his face.

Full well I remember that I was ashamed
And dared not to look on feeling that I was blamed,
Till a tale of exploits I was able to bring
That should prove well my right to step into the ring.

What a pleasure it is, for an old man to see
His son coming forward and telling how he

By his prowess has sent a dread foe to the grave,
And won for himself the proud title of brave.
His blood stirs within him like that of young men,
And he wishes to fight all his battles again.

SUMMER OCCUPATIONS

When the time of our national dance has gone by,
Our corn has been hoed, and is standing knee high,
Our young men start away toward the sunsetting glow
To hunt for the deer and the big buffalo,
And to kill any Sioux, if perchance they are found
Committing a trespass on our hunting ground.
Some go to the lead mines, while those who may wish
Go to gather mat stuff.   Others go to get fish.
Our young men bring the meat that they went to obtain,
And sometimes the scalps of Sioux men they have slain,
Because on our grounds they in trespass have been,—
Or by a Sioux band they may be driven in.
If the Sioux have killed last, before us they will flee,
But if we have killed last, then their right it must be
To press upon us, and we have to give way.
Indians fight for revenge, and seek only to slay
When their folks have been killed, or the foe has been found
Committing a trespass on their hunting ground.

The others returning bring mats, lead and fish.
Exchanges are then made to suit every wish.
This time is the happiest time of the year,
And we visit and feast with those we hold dear.
'Tis a time when we try fullest honors to show
To the Spirit who cares for all creatures below.
We feast the Great Spirit, the giver of good,
And return to him thanks as each feels that he should.
For myself, from a spring I ne'er take a drink
Without being moved of his goodness to think.
He has given us reason as truly as sight,

4

That we might distinguish the wrong from the right.
With it we determine the things we should do:
Our duty is then the right path to pursue.
If the Great Spirit wished us to be as white men,
He could easily make us all over again.

Some feast the Bad Spirit, in hopes he will cease
From his evil designs and leave them in peace.
The Good Spirit gives them no cause for alarm,
For they feel very sure he will do them no harm.

The time of our ripening corn now appears
And our young folks are anxious to pull roasting ears;
But no one is permitted to do so until
The signal is given, when all with a will
Join to make a great feast and to thank the Good One
For the gift of the corn, growing fair in the sun.

The Fall Sports of the Men While the Women Gather the Corn

When the autumn comes on we assemble to play
The Indian ball game, baggatiway.
In about equal numbers the players divide:
From three to five hundred appear on a side.
The game is for horses and blankets and guns,
Or anything else, as our property runs.
The victorious party now joyfully takes,
With the friendly consent of the losers, the stakes.
The racing of horses is then our resort,
And this we continue with other fine sport,
Till the corn is secured, and the time comes around
To prepare for our trip to the far hunting ground.

The Winter Hunt

The traders arrive with the things that we need,
Which they give us on credit, so we can proceed
To the hunt well equipped to take all sorts of game,

And bring to them later the skins of the same.
We tell them the place where our camp will be made,
And where they should locate the house for their trade.

At this house we deposit a part of our corn,
And leave our old people all jaded and worn.
The traders are kind to us all and well-willed:
No trader by Saukies has ever been killed.

We disperse in small parties to hunt here and there,
Then we bring in the skins we have taken with care.
We remain with the trader till springtime draws nigh,
Card-playing and feasting as time passes by.

Then again we go forth, some the beaver to trap,
While others seek muskrats and coons it may hap.
The rest go to sugar camps, that they may make,
What all folks delight in, the fine sugar cake.
To a place on the river our stuff we then bring,
And to-gether go up to our home in the spring.

VI. TRADITIONS AND INCIDENTS

The Origin of Corn, Beans and Tobacco

As Given by Black Hawk

I WILL now describe the means
Whereby came our corn and beans,
And tobacco, the delight
Of the red man and the white.

In the days of long ago
Two young hunters shot a doe,
And prepared as fine a roast
As the best of cooks could boast,

When descending through the air
From the clouds a woman, fair
As the dawning of the day,
Came and sat not far away.

Thinking she had smelled the meat
And desired some to eat,
In the kindness of their hearts
They brought her the choicest parts.

She upon their bounty fed
And in gracious accents said:
"Come back to this place next year.
Your reward will then be here."

Speaking thus, before their eyes
She ascended to the skies,
And the clouds, that first revealed,
Soon again her form concealed.

Then these wonder-laden men
To the village came again,
Telling these things to the tribe.
They were met with laugh and jibe.

When a year had passed away,
Quite a company one day
Went to view the place with care,
And to note what might be there.

Where her right hand touched the ground
Corn was growing all around,
And where rested her left hand
Podded beans were seen to stand.

From the place whereon she sat
Without deer-skin, robe or mat,
Grew tobacco, the delight
Of the red man and the white.

THE FRENCH VIOLINIST[17]

O the Frenchman! O the Frenchman!
O the care-free, roving Frenchman
    Of the old wild Indian days!
Here to-day and there to-morrow,
Never trouble he would borrow,
    Well he fitted Indian ways.

Such a Frenchman in the village,
In the happy Saukie village,
    Found a welcome and a home.
With his singing and his dancing,
With his leaping and his prancing,
    He was like a fabled gnome.

With his fiddle, wondrous fiddle,
With his squeaking, speaking fiddle,
    Hour by hour he entertained.

All the Saukies stood and listened,
And their eyes with pleasure glistened,
    With a joy that was unfeigned.

For some Saukies at The Tower,
At the far famed Black Hawk Tower,
    Once he played and danced and sang,
With excessive animation;
And their shouts of approbation
    Over all the valley rang.

As the Frenchman heard their shouting,
Heard their cheering and their shouting,
    Loud he made the music swell:
By their plaudits more elated,
He piroutted and gyrated —
    Backward from the cliff he fell.

Lovingly they bore his body,
Bore his broken, lifeless body
    To a grave within the dell;
And they say that on The Tower,
Yearly at that day and hour,
    Strains of music softly swell.

A Sioux-Saukie Love Tragedy[18]

This may be used as a little pageant with a reader and six Indian characters: The Young Sioux Brave, The Saukie Maiden, The Saukie Mother, The Saukie Father and The Two Saukie Brothers. Elaborate scenery is not necessary.

I

The Reader:

The tribes of the Sioux and the Saukies
    Were enemies through the long years:
The fruits of their intercourse always
    Were bloodshed and sorrow and tears.

The hunting camps of the Saukies
    Were south of the grounds of the Sioux,
And some sort of clash was expected
    Each winter ere hunting was through.

II

The young Sioux Brave is seen on the outskirts of a Sioux hunting camp.

The Young Sioux Brave:

I have slain a Saukie warrior
    And a brave henceforth am I:
That a youth may come to his manhood
    Some other man must die.[19]

As a brave I may now have a wigwam
    And live in my manhood's pride;
But ah! who shall be the maiden,
    That will come to be my bride?

Shall it be the War Chief's daughter,
    The War Chief's daughter fair,
With her eyes so soft and tender,
    And her braids of raven hair?

The Chief saw me when the Saukie
    Beneath my blow fell dead,
And he saw me tear the scalp-lock
    From his cleft and bleeding head.

She saw me in the scalp dance,
    As I leaped and bounded by,
And I think she smiled upon me
    When I waved the trophy high.

I will seek again the Saukies,
  I will go to their camp alone,
I will steal my way to a wigwam,
  And none shall hear the moan

Of the brave my knife shall slaughter.
  I will tear the scalp-lock away
And be far back on my journey,
  Before the break of the day.

And O, how the band will acclaim me
  For a deed so brave and fine!
And the War Chief's lovely daughter,
  The choice of my heart shall be mine.

III

The Saukie Maiden and her Mother are gathering sticks where the woodland meets the prairie. A severe snow storm comes on.

The Saukie Maiden:

O Mother, the storm beats fiercely,
  The wind like a wolf is wild,
And soon the white snow on the prairie
  In billowy heaps will be piled.

Let us go while we can to the wigwam:
  We have all the sticks we can bear,
And for days they will keep the fire burning
  With those that are already there.

The Saukie Mother:

Yes, daughter, I lead and you follow:
  We will make our way steady and slow;
With the wind on our right and behind us,
  We shall soon reach the wigwam, I know.

The Saukie Maiden:

> O Mother, what's that on the prairie?
>   It appears to be drawing near:
> Through the storm I can see a dim outline,—
>   'Tis a man, and a Sioux,—and he's here.

The Saukie Mother:

> You are lost, I can see, on the prairie:
>   You have strayed from some Sioux camp away;
> Though your people are always our foemen,
>   You may come to our wigwam to-day.

IV

The Saukie women and The Young Sioux Brave come to the Saukie wigwam in the hunting camp.

The Saukie Father:

> It is well.   The Sioux Brave may enter
>   And share with us in our cheer:
> A friend shall he be, not a foeman,
>   As long as the storm keeps him here.

The Young Sioux Brave:

> As I lift up the flap of your wigwam,
>   All enmity ceases to be:
> I would not be counted as foreman
>   To those who are friendly to me.

The Reader:

> No word by the maiden was spoken,
>   And demurely cast down were her eyes:
> What feelings were stirred in her bosom
>   No one may attempt to surmise.

The faces of two younger brothers
    Grew dark as they looked on the Sioux,
As though a far different greeting
    They'd extend were it theirs to do.

For the life of a man stood between them
    And the coveted title of brave;
And the chance to strike at a foeman
    Was the one they were aptest to crave.

The storm was severe and protracted,
    And before the sun shone bright above
The Sioux brave and the fair Saukie maiden
    Had quietly fallen in love.

They plighted their faith to each other,
    A faith that should outlast their breath,
That through life should keep warm their affection
    And bind them together in death.

V

The lovers part with a plan for The Young Sioux Brave
to come to Saukenauk in mid-summer for The Saukie
Maiden.

The Young Sioux Brave:

O fairest of Indian women,
    O Saukie Maid, tender and true,
You may know that I e'er will be faithful,
    You may trust in the heart of a Sioux.

To-day I must go to my people,
    While you with the campers must stay,
Till the winter season for hunting
    Shall have worn its slow moons away.

And then with the hunters and women
　　You will to your village repair,
To Saukenauk by the great river,
　　And quietly wait for me there.

I will come when the moon of midsummer
　　First shines near the bright setting sun:
O heart of my heart, from my coming
　　We two shall forever be one.

The Saukie Maiden:

You must steal from the east through the forest
　　To the end of the farthest cornfield,
Half way between noontime and sunset,—
　　O, be sure to remain well concealed.

VI

　　The lovers meet and, as a storm is approaching, flee to the overhanging rock of The Big Spring Grotto for shelter.

The Reader:

On that fateful day in midsummer
　　When The Sioux Brave came for his bride,
He found her patiently hoeing
　　In the field by her dear Mother's side.

The Mother soon went to the village:
　　When fully she'd passed out of sight,
The Brave sounded forth a sharp whistle
　　And The Maiden's heart thrilled with delight.

Not by sign nor by sound did she answer,
　　Lest his presence she might thus disclose,
But leisurely still she continued
　　Her work to the end of the rows.

How joyful then was their greeting!
  How hopeful their prospects for life
As Saukie and Sioux in one wigwam,
  From which love should forever bar strife!

But alas! against love there is hatred:
  Though hid as they thought from all view,
The brothers had noted their meeting,
  And were getting their guns to pursue.

As the lovers passed into the forest,
  The heavens grew dark overhead:
They noted a storm was approaching,
  And changing their course quickly sped

To the base of the cliff, by the river,
  That arched overhead wide and high,
And as the storm burst in its fury,
  They stood there protected and dry.

The maiden looked up to her lover,
  Her lover looked down in her face:
The wrathful brothers pursuing
  Saw him fold her in tender embrace.

That instant the lightning illumined
  All the earth with a terrible glare,
And the rattling peal of the thunder
  Broke forth on the shuddering air.

By the bolt the great cliff was shattered.
  Heart to heart the true lovers met doom:
The rock that had been their protection
  Now in fragments became their great tomb.

An Indian Prank

The Foxes needed horses,
  And after many talks
They sent a delegation
  To ask them of the Sauks.

The Sauks at once consented,
  (They thought it very fit,)
But asked the delegation
  Upon the ground to sit,

Until the willing young men
  Might approbation win
By rounding up the horses
  And swiftly riding in.

They quickly brought the horses,
  (In these the Sauks were rich,)
But every scamp among them
  Brought, too, a handsome switch.

Then round and round the circle
  They rode with all their might,
And switched the delegation
  To their own hearts' delight.

The Foxes smoked in silence,
  Nor dodged nor winced nor rose,
But took as fairest sunshine
  The stormy rain of blows.

Then suddenly dismounting,
  With manner kind and grave
To these well tested Foxes
  The Sauks their horses gave.

INDIAN JUDGMENT[20]

Chief Killic had three wives
  And might have had his ten,
But rather sought intrigues
  With wives of other men.

One of his best young braves
  Brought to his lodge a wife:
They lived in happiness
  Without a thought of strife.

One day the brave returned
  From long and fruitful chase,
And found upon the couch
  The Chieftain in his place.

He slew him then and there.
  Up from her guilty bed
The faithless wife arose,
  And to her brother fled.

The husband sought at once
  The Chieftain's eldest son,
And proffered him the knife
  With which the deed was done.

Then baring his broad breast
  He stood with manly air,
As saying without words,
  " 'Tis your place to strike there."

"Think not," the son replied,
  "That you alone are brave:
I, too, have shame to hide,—
  I'm ready for the grave."

The husband's brother then
  In his turn took the knife
And pierced the son's brave heart,
  Continuing the strife.

When eight man had gone down,
  The Chiefs held back the hand
Of Death, lest none should be
  Left living of that band.

Beside the village then
  A wedge-shaped grave was made,
And in its narrow depths
  The faithless wife was laid.

Upon the living form
  Of this unworthy bride
They placed her paramour
  And husband side by side.

Above him in his turn
  They put each noble brave,
Whose act to expiate
  Had brought him to the grave.

With soil of Mother Earth
  They spread the bodies o'er,
And turf to heal the gash
  She on her bosom bore.

A "DIFFICULTY" BETWEEN THE SAUKS AND THE IOWAS

Black Hawk's Account

Our young warriors again and again
Had killed some of the Iowa men.
For these breaches we had made amends
By the sending of gifts to their friends;

But at our last council with them
We said we would surely condemn
Any one of our tribe who should slay
An Iowa, and no delay
Should follow till into their hands
He should go to meet their demands.

Though the matter was fully explained
To our warriors, they were not restrained;
But next winter an Iowa brave
By a Saukie was brought to his grave.

As soon as the breach became known,
Our young man was called on to atone
With his life for the life of the slain,
Lest the nation in shame should remain.

Though sick, he was willing to go,
But his brother, insistent, said, "No.
He can't travel.   'Twould be a disgrace.
I am ready to go in his place."

With the brother we started that day
To the Iowa village, away
A week's journey, and when we drew nigh
We halted and bade him good bye.

He went with a step firm and strong,
Singing bravely and loud his death song,
To the village and sat in the square,
That was formed by the wigwams set there.

Then one of the Chiefs came to us.
After greetings we spoke to him thus:
"Our promise has now been fulfilled:
The brother of our brave, who killed
Your warrior, has come in his stead:

(For the slayer is on a sick bed:)
In your village he sings his death song,
Prepared to atone for the wrong."

Having spoken, without more delay
We mounted and rode fast away.
When the dews of the evening fell damp,
We halted and went into camp.

As we were preparing to eat,
We heard the low, rythmical beat
Of horses hoofs coming with speed.
Not knowing what might be our need,
And used as we were to alarms,
We sprang to our feet and to arms.

But, behold, 'twas our young Saukie brave,
Whom we thought no power could save
From the wrath of the Iowa band,
That had just received him from our hand.

He told us that after we left,
He felt he was wholly bereft.
The Iowa braves gathered around
The place where he sat on the ground
And, shaking their clubs and their spears,
Endeavored to work on his fears.
O'er and o'er with most violent breath
They threatened to put him to death.

But after this show of their heat
They brought to him something to eat;
Then they sat down with him on the ground
And the peace pipe was passed all around.
Then they greeted him as a true brave,
And as Iowas, to him they gave
Two horses and presents beside,
And told him to mount and to ride

With such speed as he needed to make,
To the end that he might overtake
His friends where they camped for the night.
He complied with the greatest delight.

When we at our village arrived
With our brave, who had not been deprived
Of his life by the Iowa band,
But had been given back to our hand,
Our people were all overjoyed
And great words of praise they employed
For the Iowas' generous deed,
And so well to its worth they gave heed,
That no Iowa since has been killed
By our nation with gratitude filled.

VII. SOME OBSERVATIONS ON
GREATNESS

IN all times, through ability, effort or fate,
  Some men have so lived as to be counted great.
Degrees in their greatness we often may note,
And sometimes we attempt to determine by vote
In what grade any great of the present or past,
Greater great, lesser great or mere great shall be classed.
Then we have a sub-class for those under the line:
We call them "near great" and think that very fine.

The great have sometimes made their advent in groups,
And the near great as often have followed in troops:
There are soldiers and statemen and singers of songs,
And others to whom meed of greatness belongs.

Sometimes a lone man in his greatness will tower
Peculiarly fit for the needs of the hour,
Like his country's own father, the great Washington,
Who a place in the heart of all peoples has won,
Or Lincoln who wrought with a spirit so brave
That no spot upon earth can be found for a slave.

Sometimes the great men have come forward in pairs,
Together to make their impress on affairs.
A Hamilton's work was indeed better done
Because balanced by that of a great Jefferson;
And the battle smoke gone, in clear light we may see
The greatness of Grant and the greatness of Lee.

Among unlettered tribes, who not much can note down,
There is small chance for any to gain wide renown;
And except as with civilized man they're in touch
Can the great ones among them be well known as such.

The Indians, unique and pursued by hard fate,
Have not failed to produce those who truly were great:
In Virginia, the Emperor-Chief, Powhatan,
The uncertain friend of the bold Englishman;
And his brother, the dread Opechancanough,
His treacherous, bloody, implacable foe,
The first one who carefully plotted and planned
To kill all the whites or drive them from the land.

In New England were two, who were father and son:
Massasoit, the kindly, benevolent one,
Who made terms with the whites, that in spite of all fears,
Were kept by both parties for fifty long years;
And King Philip, who gathered the men of his race
To destroy all the whites, or drive them in disgrace
Across the broad waters o'er which they had come
And preserve this great land as the Indian's home;
But who met such defeat that the Indian power
In New England was broken from his dying hour.

And many another great name there appears
In the annals of red men through following years.
Of these that of Pontiac, Ottawa Chief,
Stands out, it is said, in the boldest relief;
Though the Shawnee, Tecumseh, some folks think to be
As a master of men even greater than he.
Each formed a great league, and with courage each fought
To drive out the whites, but their work came to naught.

The Sauks' contribution to greatness appears
In two Chieftains, whose fame will pass on through the
        years,
Each one a brave man and each one a true Sac:[21]
Great Mek-a-tai-me-she-ki-ah-ki-ak,
Or the Black Sparrow Hawk, who was fain to contend
For what he thought was right to the bitterest end;
And the broad-minded Keokuk, who could foresee
That a peaceful adjustment far better would be.

BLACK HAWK

From painting by James Byrd King

VIII.   THE EARLY LIVES OF BLACK HAWK AND KEOKUK[22]

BLACK HAWK

BLACK HAWK was born in Rock Island
    In seventeen sixty and seven
A lineal descendent of Thunder,
    Who brought down the lightning from heaven.[23]

His father was Pyesa, warrior
    And medicine man of his tribe,[24]
To whom all the Indian virtues
    The son is most glad to ascribe.

As a lad he wounded a foeman:
    Thenceforth he was classed with the braves,[25]
To follow the path of a warrior
    And line it with enemies graves.

.　.　.　.　.　.

Soon after, before he was fifteen,
    A Chief of the Muscow tribe came
For recruits to go 'gainst the Osages
    And win for themselves greater fame.

Black Hawk, with the band, saw his father
    Strike a mighty antagonist dead,
And with the deft hand of an expert
    Tear away the scalp-lock from his head.

The bloody sight roused his ambition:
    With valor he rushed on a foe,
And swinging his tomahawk stoutly
    He smote him to earth with a blow

Then he ran his lance through the body,
   Took the scalp and returned to his place
By the side of his sire, who said nothing
   But had a pleased look on his face.

The enemy in this engagement
   Lost many.   The Saukies with joy
Returned to their town for a scalp dance,—
   One warrior who danced was a boy.

* * * * * *

When a few moons had passed the young Black Hawk,
   At the head of a party of eight
Made attack on one hundred Osages,
   As though he would tempt even fate.

One man he laid low, and his comrades
   Took the scalp, while he found out the strength
Of the foemen in arms and equipment.
   It was great, and he drew off at length.

* * * * * *

For this feat he was greatly applauded,
   And he found himself able to raise
A force of one hundred and eighty,
   In the course of about twenty days.

They left Saukenauk in high spirits,
   Determined that they would not fail:
When near the great river Missouri
   They struck their old enemies' trail,

And followed with care to the village
   Expecting to find them all there;
But the fearful Osages had scattered,
   Unwilling the danger to dare.

The Saukies were so disappointed
   That all but five braves left for home:[26]
Then Black Hawk thanked the Great Spirit
   For the five really brave who had come.

The little band found it was needful
   Great caution indeed to employ,
But after some days they succeeded
   In killing one man and a boy

For a small band, by others deserted,
   They thought they had done very well;
And bearing the scalps as a trophy
   They went home the story to tell.

. . . . . .

Because of this mutinous conduct,
   Although not considered to blame,
A large force he could not assemble
   For the field, till his nineteenth year came.

The Osages by stealth had committed
   Full many outrages betimes:
Black Hawk gathered two hundred warriors
   To punish them well for their crimes.

They went to the enemies country,
   Where they faced a force large as their own
And engaged in a desperate battle,
   In which no quarter was shown.

With his own hand the brave Saukie leader,
   Determined a record to make,
Killed and scalped five warrior Osages,
   And killed also a squaw by mistake.

The Osages were badly defeated,
   With a loss of one hundred in all,
While out of the ranks of the Saukies
   'Twas the fortune of nineteen to fall.

So sadness was mixed with rejoicing,
   As bearing their scalps they came back;
But for many long moons the Osages
   On their hunting grounds left not a track.

     . . . . .

The Cherokees, so said the Saukies,
   Their women and children decoyed
From their homes, with the one dreadful purpose
   That each of them might be destroyed.

At the head of a brave little party,
   Old Pyesa, valiant and wise,
When down to the Merrimac country[27]
   These villainous men to chastise.

When they reached there a much larger party.
   Of Cherokee warriors drew nigh:
Old Pyesa in an engagement
   Went down with a wound in his thigh.

Black Hawk then became the Commander
   And fought with such desperate fire,
That the Cherokee forces fell backward
   And at last were compelled to retire.

Twenty-eight of their warriors had fallen,
   (Of whom the Brave Black Hawk slew three,)
Six Saukies and Pyesa also,
   For his wound had proved fatal to be.

By the death of his father, the Black Hawk
　　To the medicine bag became heir:
He took it, and buried with sorrow
　　The body of Pyesa there.

. . . . . .

Because of his fearful misfortune,
　　In humble apparel arrayed
And with face painted black as the midnight,
　　For five years he fasted and prayed.

The Great Spirit saw and took pity,
　　And when the Osages again
Began their malicious aggressions,
　　He gathered a band of brave men,

And sought to engage them in battle;
　　But they quickly abandoned the ground,
And though the brave Saukies pursued them,
　　Only six of their number were found.

Black Hawk forebore to destroy them,
　　But, making them prisoners, took
Them down to the post at Saint Louis,
　　That the Spanish might bring them to book.

. . . . . .

But so dastardly were the Osages,
　　And such injuries had been received
By the Saukies, that Black Hawk determined
　　Their destruction should now be achieved.

He recruited of Saukies and Foxes
　　Five hundred, and Iowa braves
One hundred: with these he expected
　　The Osages to bring to their graves.

Having traveled for days they discovered
　A trail the Osages had made:
Then they went into camp and awaited
　The morrow to make sudden raid.

Quite early they started, ere sunset
　Their purpose was partly fulfilled;
For the dwellers in full forty lodges,
　Excepting two squaws, had been killed.

Seven men and two boys had fallen
　Beneath the Black Hawk's trusty blade,
And, as a side issue, the women
　By him had been prisoners made.

The Osages lost many brave warriors,
　Which caused those remaining to cease
Their bold and outrageous aggressions
　On the Saukies and leave them in peace.

　　　　　.　.　.　.　.　.

Black Hawk ever mourned for his father,
　And sought direst vengeance to take
Upon the whole Cherokee nation
　That he hated for Pyesa's sake.

So bitter indeed was his feeling,
　Beyond any hope to describe,
That he wished the annihilation
　Of the very last one of the tribe.

Recruiting another war party
　He sought them, but found only five,
So few that in spite of his hatred,
　He concluded to leave them alive.

Four of these they released, but still mindful
  Of the purpose for which they had come,
They retained one squaw as a trophy
  And took her with them to their home.

· · · · ·

They were soon called again into warfare,
  Their own grounds for hunting to save
From the Chippewas, crafty Osages
  And Kaskaskias, valiant and brave.

In the war there were seven hard battles
  And many a skirmish beside,
Before the invaders were driven
  From the Sauk and Fox hunting ground wide.

The slain of the foe were in hundreds,
  From the various divisions and bands:
Of these thirteen of the bravest
  Had been killed by the Black Hawk's own hands.

· · · · ·

The close of the war found the Black Hawk
  Just ending his thirty-fifth year,
A well proven warrior and leader,
  Without a reproach or a fear.

He stood at five feet and ten inches,
  And was slender, but straight and well made;
His features were long in their outline,
  His complection a dark even shade.

He was modest and quiet in manner,
  And had no great taste for display;
But a dignity fitting his station
  In his bearing was noted alway.

He was in full measure an Indian
  And loved the old Indian life,
With its seasonal round of rude pleasures
  And its quota of warfare and strife.

Intolerant, poetic, devoted,
  Patriotic, impatient of change,
His life was deep in its purpose,
  But not quite so wide in its range.

KEOKUK

Great Keokuk, Chief of the Saukies,
  First opened his eyes to the light
In a wigwam beside the Rock River
  That flashes its waters so bright

By the site of the old Indian village,
  As Saukenauk known at that time,
But now as a part of Rock Island,
  And there he attained to his prime.

The time of his fortunate coming
  Was seventeen eighty and eight:
His parents were ranked with the humble,
  As is often the case with the great.

He was known as a lover of horses:
  He could judge them and train them and ride,
Before he emerged from his boyhood,
  In a way to give any one pride.

.   .   .   .   .

He grew up and matured very early:
  At fifteen he was sturdy and strong,

KEOKUK ON HORSEBACK

Painted from life by George Catlin. The original painting is in the National Museum at Washington, D. C.

b

With all the essential endowments,
    That to a full manhood belong.

At that time he went with the warriors
    Of his tribe to fight the great Sioux,
Well mounted and fully accoutered
    Some deed of a great daring to do.

Then one of the Sioux braves, observing
    With covetous vision, drew near,
Determined to slay the young warrior
    And thus gain the horse and the gear.

The Saukie boy seeing him coming,
    Read clearly the thought of his mind,
And holding his lance in position
    Dashed forward with speed of the wind.

The fighting was done with great fury,
    Each one was called on for his best,
But the Sioux brave fell from his charger
    With the lance of the Sauk in his breast.

The Sioux were the best of good horsemen
    And to slay one when mounted, in fight,
Was considered an act of great prowess,
    Which the Sauks all acclaimed with delight.

They esteemed it a national triumph:
    In its honor a great feast they gave,
And to Keokuk gladly accorded
    The rank of an eminent brave.

As a further mark of distinction
    They gave him the right to appear
On horseback at all public meetings,
    A right he considered most dear.

When a few years had passed the young warrior
    By the usual method was made
An Eagle or brave of the last fire,
    A subordinate Chief of fourth grade.[28]

At twenty-four years he was War Chief:
    How made so will later be told.
In discharging the duties of office,
    He was faithful, sagacious and bold.

.   .   .   .   .   .

When crossing a plain with his warriors,
    On a hunting trip in the fall,
A party of Sioux came upon them
    With a war-whoop designed to appall.

The Sioux exceeded in number,
    But Keokuk ordered, not flight
Nor advance toward the oncoming forces
    To engage in a general fight,

But instead he directed his warriors
    To dismount with all possible speed,
And with horses arranged in a circle,
    To his further commands to give heed.

Standing thus behind living breastworks
    They waited till Sioux braves came nigher,
Then into their ranks with precision
    They poured forth a death-dealing fire.

The fierce Sioux retired in disorder,
    But attempted again and again,
By force of superior number
    To ride down the brave Saukie men.

Each attempt resulted in losses
    And, taking their wounded and slain,
They finally gave up the effort
    And sadly withdrew o'er the plain.

.   .   .   .   .   .

On another occasion in autumn,
    The Sauks going forth to the hunt,
Here and there in small parties had scattered
    According to Indian wont.

In the meantime the women and children,
    (Except for the boys and old men
Without any kind of protection,)
    Were awaiting their coming again.

Toward night from a high elevation
    Near the line dividing their lands,
Chief Keokuk and a small party
    Saw the Sioux in gathering bands,

About to engage in a war dance.
    They knew that it meant an attack
On their village, ere they could join forces
    And to the defenceless go back.

In an instant the great Chief determined
    To visit the war dance alone
And frighten the Sioux from a purpose,
    That a real man could never condone.

He then directed his warriors
    To remain where they were for an hour:
They might know in that time if he came not
    He was in the dread enemy's power.

Some were then to make haste to the village
  And give warning to scatter and hide,
While others should gather the warriors
  And thus a resistance provide.

But if they should hear his own war-whoop,
  With full force they were to respond,
To mount and rush forward to meet him
  And if needful to go far beyond.

Then he rode in the gathering darkness
  Toward the Sioux camp, to meet the great need;
When he came within hailing distance
  He put spurs to his mettlesome steed.

The horse sped on like a rocket.
  When the Sioux heard the sound of its feet,
And saw it flash out of the darkness,
  Their surprise and dismay were complete.

In an instant a pathway was opened
  Through the ranks of the war-crazy host:
Great Keokuk dashed to the center,
  And made a quick halt at the post.

, There he sat, like a Knight on his charger,
  And demanded in thunderous tone,
That the War Chief should stand up before him
  As one who for crime must atone.

Then he said: "Do you know there are traitors
  Or enemies here in your band,
Who have told me the cowardly project
  That you and your tribe have in hand,—

"To make war on our women and children
  While myself and my braves are away,
To steal on them like beasts of the forest
  And pillage and capture and slay?

"It may be that these people are liars:
   I should hate to think you were so low;
But if they speak truth, haughty War Chief,
   I want you and your warriors to know,

"That the Sauks are prepared to receive you.
   If you to our village draw nigh,
For every pappoose that is injured
   Some Sioux man among you must die."

As the arrow that springs from the bowstring
   Speeds away on its course to the mark,
Bold Keokuk, wheeling his charger,
   Sped away on his course through the dark.

The Sioux braves gathered their senses
   In the vacuum left in his place,
And flinging themselves on their ponies
   They started in resolute chase

Then the brave and masterly Saukie
   Slackened speed with a touch of the rein,
And led at safe distance the Sioux men
   Where he would in a course o'er the plain.

As he neared the place of his warriors
   He sent his war-whoop on the air;
The response came with thunderous volume
   To show all the Saukies were there.

The Sioux forces bravely pursuing,
   Were startled and filled with affright,
And suddenly wheeling their ponies
   They took to inglorious flight.

Chief Keokuk leading his handful,
   Who yelled like a thousand or more,
Having made the desired impression,
   All further pursuing gave o'er.

The Sioux then abandoned their project
  And to their own village went back,
In order to make preparation
  To resist any Saukie attack.

. . . . .

Though brave, as a warrior in battle,
  And wise, as War Chief in command,
It is for his courage and wisdom
  In peace, he is known through the land.

He stood at five feet and eight inches,
  And was strongly and stockily made;
His features were rounded in outline,
  His color a light copper shade.

He was dignified in demeanor,
  Very fond of barbaric array,
And loved to have round him attendants
  To make a still further display.

An Indian Chief by his merit,
  He was wedded to Indian ways;
And by choice he followed their customs
  In full to the end of his days.

Magnanimous, practical, hopeful,
  Patriotic, but mindful of facts:
His regard for humanity's welfare
  Was abundantly proved by his acts.

IX. THE COURSE OF EVENTS

THE ENGLISHMEN AND THE COLONISTS IN THEIR ATTITUDE TOWARD THE INDIANS

THE Englishmen had no desire to possess
    The whole of the land to the natives distress.
The country was wide and but scantily filled
And a very small part of it only was tilled.
If the Indians were willing to cease from their strife
And make an approach to a civilized life,
There was plenty of room for both white men and red,—
They could traffic and trade and do well, so they said.

The Colonists found a hard task at their hands
To makes homes for themselves in the new and wild lands,
That they by some sort of treaties had bought;
And as is well known there were times when they fought
With the savage red men, the lords of the land
Who the terms of the bargain did not understand.

THE FRENCH AND INDIAN WAR

Colonial charters claimed the western lands
Beyond the mountains to the far sea sands;
But France as firmly claimed the valley wide
Through which the Mississippi pours its tide.

The issue did not turn on abstract right,
Or on the question of superior might,
Nor yet on language, which would be more fit
As name to give a fort, "Du Quesne" or "Pitt";

But rather on the use that should be made
Of these broad lands, for settlement or trade,
For homesteads and industrial employ,
Or scattered outposts and *coureur du bois*.

In seventeen fifty-four the war begun[29]
With Jumonville's defeat by Washington.
It ran its bloody course for weary years
Of varied fortunes, hopes and doubts and fears,

Of dreadful Indian raids and massacres,[30]
As every record of the time avers,
Till Wolfe went up the Heights of Abraham
And won in death a vict'ry o'er Montcalm.

'Twas later in beginning o'er the sea,
And peace was not declared till sixty-three:
A treaty then gave these contested lands[31]
And all of Canada to British hands.

The British Attitude Toward the Colonists and the Beginning of the Revolution

Short-sighted Britain, jealous of her own,
Who for self government a taste had shown,
Determined to restrain the settlers bold,
And under close control these lands to hold,

As hunting grounds for Indians, from whose trade
Additions to her income might be made.
Ink on the treaty being dry, her word
Was issued in the name of George the Third:[32]

"Know ye, our loving subjects, that our will
And pleasure is, which you should all fulfill,
That western lands shall be the Indians' home,
Where they as hunters far and near may roam.

"You must abide this side the water-shed
Or suffer under our displeasure dread,
Except as we to some of you may give
A special leave upon these lands to live."

The loving subjects did not seem inclined
In this regard their loving King to mind,
But freely passed beyond the mountains' crest
To make them homes within the central west.

Thus England came to take the Frenchman's stand,
The while her Colonists still sought for land,
On which to build those institutions strong
That to a state of civil life belong.

. . . . . .

In seventy-four the Parliament passed
A measure they thought would be certain at last
The Colonists' plans for expansion to check,
By including these lands as a part of Quebec.

The people were nursing their grievances sore[33]
And this to their minds seemed to be but one more.
Rebellion was ripe and repression meant war,
For both sides felt assured there was reason therefor.

It began in due time and was waged for a year
When, wishing to make all the issues more clear,
The people a national banner unfurled
And submitted their facts to an on-looking world.

Among the bad deeds they ascribed to the King
They carefully cited his efforts to bring
The merciless savages 'gainst the frontier,
Whose known rule of war, as the records appear,
Is an undistinguished destruction of all
Who into their terrible power may fall.

Throughout the long contest the King did employ
Against his own people the dread Iroquois,
And other tribes too of the North and North-west,
Who willingly came at his cruel behest.

Indeed there were British commanders, 'tis said
Who paid for each scalp from a colonist's head.
Chief of these was one Hamilton, who at Detroit
Rewarded each band for its fearful exploit.[34]

George Rogers Clark and the Conquest of the North West

No bolder man has ever made his mark
On hist'ry's pages than George Rogers Clark.
His courage and initiative won
Momentous vic'tries over Hamilton.[35]
By means that every manly man commends
He awed the Indians, made the Frenchmen friends,
And largely helped to gain the West as part
Of this new nation from the very start.

Himself conceived the plan, and with the aid
Of Patrick Henry his arrangements made.[36]
With scarce two hundred men he marched away
And, taking by surprise Kaskaskia,
Without the firing of a single gun
The village and the fort were quickly won.
Then on Cahokia he made demands
And that place also fell into his hands.[37]

He called the Indian Chiefs of many tribes
And, without presents, flattery or bribes,
He bluntly told them what he came there for
And bade them make their choice of peace or war.

With such a man they did not care to fight,
But quickly took from him the belt of white.
The Pottawatomies and Chippeways,
Sacks, Foxes, Puans, Sayges, Ottaways[38]
And many others gladly grasped his hand
And gave him welcome to the western land.

By friendly efforts of the Priest, Gibault,
Vincennes was taken on without assault;[39]
And through the Grand Gate, old Tobacco's son,
The confidence of Indians there was won.

When Hamilton had heard of these events
He planned at once an action of offense,
By which he hoped these places to regain
And royal rule thenceforward to maintain.

He led two hundred men o'er lake and fens
And down the Wabash into old Vincennes.[40]
The fort surrendered. As the flag came down
The French renewed allegiance to the crown.

So far so good, the work had been well done,
But winter then was on, and Hamilton
Thought best to make repairs, and in the spring
To capture Fort Kaskaskia for his King.

. . . . . .

Over six weeks had passed before a report
Had reached Colonel Clark of the fall of the fort.[41]
Perceiving at once how great was the need
For immediate action, he marshaled with speed
A force of one hundred and seventy men,
Inspired them all with his spirit, and then
Marched away in the cold and the rain and the mud,
Waded through the drowned lands and passed over the
flood,
Assaulted and captured the fort, and writ down
In the book of great deeds one of greatest renown.[42]

'Twas the sum of his deeds that enabled great Jay,
At the council of peace in diplomacy's day,
To hold back from England and France and Spain
For the new-born nation, this great domain.[43]

Spain Enters the War—Raids and Counter Raids

To be neighborly, and her own cause to advance,
Spain entered the war in alliance with France.[44]
On the sea and at home she had much on her hands,
And little attempted in these western lands.
The post at Saint Joseph was won in a raid,
But no plan or effort to hold it was made.

. . . . . .

Captain Sinclair of Mackinac sent out a force
Of British and Indians, to follow a course
To the Saint Louis country the posts to annoy,
And if possible capture and loot and destroy.[45]

The British were few, and were under command
Of one Captain Hesse,—the Indian band,
That was mainly relied on to make the attacks,
Very largely consisted of Foxes and Sacs.[46]

They failed in their efforts and soon started back,
But the Spaniards and Long Knives were hot on their track,
Destroying all Indian crops that they found[47]
And burning each village quite down to the ground.

When they reached Saukenauk the Indian band
Determined to make a last desperate stand,
But defeat and retreat ill-prepared them for fight,
And though double in numbers they soon took to flight,
While the Spaniards and Long Knives with torches in hand,
Destroyed their fair village and laid waste their land.

In seventeen eighty these events took place.
Black Hawk, the coming champion of his race,
Was then a lad of thirteen, but this war
He makes no mention of in his memoir.

SOME BATTLES WITH THE INDIANS FOLLOWING
THE REVOLUTIONARY WAR

The war being over, the settlers with zest
And in much larger numbers poured into The West.
The British were slow in surrendering forts
According to treaty, along the lake ports;
But by gifts and intrigue every effort they made
To hold Indian friendship and Indian trade.

The settlers and Indians were often at strife,
That resulted sometimes in a sad loss of life.
General Harmon was sent with an army to meet
With the Indian forces, but suffered defeat
In the first of three battles, all fated to be
Most bitterly fought near the River Maumee.
The next year the Governor, General St. Clair,
In an effort the cause of the whites to repair,
Marched against the red men with a much larger force,
But was ambushed, and met a defeat that was worse.[48]

It was left for General "Mad Anthony" Wayne
To win the third fight, and prestige to regain.
All the Indian Chiefs soon were pleading for peace,
And from rapine and blood there was welcome surcease.
A treaty was made and possessory rights
To three-fourths of Ohio were given the whites.[49]

THE LOUISIANA PURCHASE

For thirty-eight years the Spaniards had held
  The trans-Mississippi lands:
Napoleon nodded, and they were returned
  Into the Frenchmen's hands.

The treaty was secret, as was the one
  In seventeen sixty-two:
And the great First Consul could do with them
  Whatever he chose to do.

He needed funds more than far-off lands,
   And he wanted to gain a friend;
For a war with Britain was sure to begin
   Whenever a war would end.

So he offered the lands to the U. S. A.,
   Those lands across the sea:
They "took him up," and the deal was closed
   In eighteen hundred three.[50]

He sold the lands for a golden song
   Of fifteen million notes,
And the chorus of that song resounds
   From a hundred million throats.

This purchase stirred the nation's pride
And, putting diff'rences aside,
All joined of their domain to boast,
Which soon must reach from coast to coast.

The President, great Jefferson,
Rejoicing in what peace had won,
Prepared at once to meet demands
For governing the new-bought lands,
And planned to send explorers forth
Far to the west, north-west and north.

The Northern District was combined
With Indiana, and consigned
To William Henry Harrison,
As Governor, who well had done
The work as such on one frontier,
Without partiality or fear.

It was the plan of government
To bring about relinquishment
Of titles by the tribes and bands
Of Indians to eastern lands,
And gradually to have "Poor Lo"
Beyond the Mississippi go.[51]

X. THE SAUKS IN DIRECT TOUCH WITH THE AMERICANS

BLACK HAWK'S ACCOUNT OF HIS VISIT TO ST. LOUIS AT THE TIME OF THE TRANSFER OF GOVERNMENT

ON my last visit to our Spanish father,
    It was a very sad and gloomy day.
They said Americans would take the country:
    The Spanish father needs must go away.

My band and I were overcome with sorrow,
    We'd always heard Americans were bad.
It made us sad to lose our Spanish father,
    Whose counsel and whose friendship we had had.

We called upon him for a farewell visit,
    For well we knew no use it was to stay.
Americans came in to see him also:
    When they appeared we quickly went away.

We found our boats and started for our village
    To tell of strangers, who had come in room
Of our beloved and gen'rous Spanish father:
    Our people heard the news in deepest gloom.

THE SAUK AND FOX TREATY OF 1804

In June of the year eighteen hundred and four
A messenger came to the Governor's door,
Bearing word from the President for him to meet
With Chiefs of the Sacs and the Foxes, and treat
With them for the cession of part of their lands,
And give in return to the Sac and Fox bands
In annual payments such goods as should be
Well suited to them, and as they might agree.

The call was sent out, and the Chieftains came down
To meet in Saint Louis, the great business town,
Where after debates and discussions were heard
The treaty was signed on November the third.[52]

The lands that by means of this treaty were got
Are shown forth in outline herewith in a plot.
Excepting the principal town, Saukenauk,
They little were used by the Fox or the Sauk.
Other tribes occupied quite a part of the same,
And the deed that was made was a sort of quit claim.
The payments were fixed at a thousand a year,—
Rather small, even then, as to us would appear.

In Article Seven provision was made
That besides the annual amount to be paid
The Indians might live on and hunt o'er these lands,
While they should remain in the government's hands.

An Indian murderer lay in the jail
At Saint Louis.   The Indians wished without fail
And at any expense to secure his release,
Which inclined them the more to a treaty of peace.
But on their return they declared he was led
To the door of the prison, and then was shot dead.[53]

The Indians admitted a sale to the south,
But never a rod above Rock River's mouth;
While not for a moment had they even thought
That their own Saukenauk had been bartered or bought.

LIEUTENANT ZEBULON M. PIKE'S REPORT CON-
CERNING THE SACS AND FOXES HE MET
ON HIS TRIP UP THE MISSISSIPPI

In eighteen hundred five an expeditionary force
Was sent to trace the mighty Mississippi to its source.
The dauntless Pike was in command, and well he did his
        part:

A record of the trip was kept, well-written from the start.[54]
From which we here note down some of the things he had
     to say
About the Sacs and Foxes that he met with on his way.[55]

The fifth day out they saw a band of Saukies spearing fish,
The spoon-bill or the bone-less cat or call-it-what-you-wish.
They gave them bread and whiskey; and the Saukies, well
     inclined,
Gave them some fish and told them where the channel they
     could find.

The ninth day out they passed a camp of Indians on the
     east,
Who fired guns.   They gave no heed, and soon the firing
     ceased.
The next day they repaired their boat.   Some Indians
     passing by
Gave them a civil greeting, but they made them no reply.

When part way up the rapids of Des Moines they met a
     band[56]
Of nineteen Sacs and two white men, who brought them
     safe to land
Above the swirling waters, at a place now called Nauvoo,
The Agricultural Station then, where Sacs were taught to do
The work of farmers, by a man named Ewing, bright and
     bold,
Whose effort has been praised, but whose success has not
     been told.

Across the river dwelt the Sacs, where Montrose is to-day.
Their Chiefs and head men came in boats to hear what
     Pike might say,
For he was charged with message to Indians far and near.
The purport of his speech he gives, and we present it here:

"Your Father, President, desires
To be acquainted with the fires
    That glow throughout the land
That he has bought; and he has sent
Young warriors forth to represent
Him, hoping all will be content
    To take them by the hand.

"He asks of us as we proceed
Of every tribe to find the need,
    That he may it supply.
If you should wish, plans will be laid
To put up here a place of trade
Where various goods may be displayed,
    And you may sell and buy.

"The murder on the stream below
Has saddened all our hearts, you know.
    We always mourn the dead;
But you assure me every one
That by your tribe it was not done,
And I have writ to Washington
    The thing that you have said.

"Your treaty states you'll apprehend
Unlicensed traders, to the end
    That they may be put out.
I can not now examine men,
But in the spring I'll come again
And I will deal with traders then,
    If any are about.

"I will be pleased if you'll agree
To send to other towns with me
    A young man in my boat,
Who by my side may stand to greet
Your friends and brothers we shall meet
And help me to my work complete
    And all I say to note."

He then presented gifts to them, tobacco, whiskey, knives,
The things on which it then was thought a mutual friend-
  ship thrives.
The Saukies listened to the speech with most profound
  respect,
And very carefully they made reply to this effect:

"We who are here and our young men
  And all our nation too
Are very glad that you have come,
  Good things for us to do.

"We're glad you think so well of us
  And of our good intent,
And for the written word that you
  To Washington have sent.

"We can not say if this would be
  The best place for a mart:
Our Saukie tribe is very great,
  And we are but a part.

"If you'll consent to stay with us
  Until to-morrow day,
We'll send a young man with you when
  You go upon your way.

"For these things you have given us
  We thank you much, indeed.
We surely prize them, and we know
  That they will meet a need."

Lieutenant Pike had great desire to be upon his way,
So after writing to his friends he left that very day.
Where Burlington is now, he thought a fine site for a fort.
An incident that there occurred he tells in his report.
Upon the river near they met four Indians and two squaws,

And, thinking to obtain some meat, concluded to make
    pause.
They gave the Indians bread and salt, "made whiskey," and
    expressed[57]
Desire for venison, but the reds were not at all impressed.
Indeed they seemed to be a very stupid little band:
They shook their heads and tried to show they did not
    understand.
No sooner had the white men gone, than these same stupid
    reds
Became hilarious and brandished hams above their heads,
While their derisive laughs were borne in cadence on the
    wind,
Till to the white men's great relief they were left far behind.

Somewhere below the river Rock they met with two canoes
Of Indians who loudly greeted them with how d'you dos
And, quickly putting to the shore, made signs for them to
    stay,
But they, not having time for that, continued on their way.

They passed the river Rock and made their camp upon the
    lands
That lay in beauty to the north where Davenport now
    stands.
Next morn they took their breakfast with a trader named
    James Aird,
Who coming down the rapids with his goods had illy fared.
He told them of the Saukie town back from Rock River's
    mouth,
And how it once had been destroyed by soldiers from the
    south.

Next day they reached a village of the Foxes, who were
    kind.
From this place they set forth again before a spanking wind.

When at Dubuque an interesting story they were told
About a company of Puants, Sacs and Foxes bold,[58]
About two hundred strong, who had gone up to make attack
Upon Sateurs. Their Chief had dreamed, and they were
      coming back.[59]

On his return Lieutenant Pike met with an officer
Who had been sent among the Sauks and Foxes to confer
About some Osage prisoners, whose freedom was desired;
But all the Sauks at Saukenauk by spirits seemed inspired.
They would not hold a conference, but said that bad white
      men
Had killed their relatives and friends and came to kill
      again.
The Captain's plume they took to be a sign of bloody war,
Which, putting feathers on, they said that they were ready
      for.

Lieutenant Pike was deeply stirred by Captain Many's tale
And said that by a *coup de main* he'd punish without fail
These scoundrels, but his orders would not let him do the
      deed:
He must continue on his way, and make the utmost speed.

Again he stopped at E. A. S. or what is now Nauvoo,[60]
And there he met two gentlemen, named Maxwell and
      Blondeau.
The Saukies at the Lower Town, that was across the way,
Were all intoxicated or "as drunk as Lords" that day.
They'd stolen from the E. A. S. a horse, a faithful hack,
Which they for liquor, that alone, were willing to bring
      back.
Lieutenant Pike, from Maxwell took a deposition strong
Concerning this delinquency, then made his way along.

The next day they met four canoes of Sauks, who wished a
      trade
Of pigeons they had taken for some liquor might be made.
7

Lieutenant Pike was much incensed at this act of the band,
And very quickly showed to them the back of his right hand.

Indeed so insolent, he says, these scoundrels came to be
Through influence of the traders that nought but the lenity[61]
Of Government, and pity for them kept him from affray,
And carrying some of their towns upon his downward way.

Black Hawk's Account of Lieutenant Pike's Visit to Saukenauk

Some time after we had lost our Spanish Father,
Up the river in a boat with some attendants,
Came a Chief, a young American Lieutenant,
Later known as General Pike, a noble warrior.

When at length this Chief arrived at Rocky River,
On the shore he came with his own talk-explainer.
He addressed us in a speech and gave us presents:
In return we gave to him of our provisions.

We were pleased with the address of this young Chieftain:
Good advice he gave, and said that our new Father
Would be sure to treat us well; and he presented
To us a new banner, which at once we hoisted.[62]

He then asked us to haul down the British colors,
Also to give up to him our British medals,
Promising to send us others from Saint Louis.
We refused because we wished to have two fathers.

When the young Chief started, we sent runners
To the village of the Foxes, some miles distant,
Asking them to treat him well when he should call there,
Which they did.   He then proceeded up the river
To head waters, thence returning to Saint Louis.
For some time no more Americans came to us,
But we were supplied with goods by British traders.

DIXON'S FERRY

General Atkinson's Headquarters in the Black Hawk War

FORT MADISON

The first structure built by white men in Iowa

d

We were fortunate in holding to our medals,
For we later were informed by our own traders
That the Chiefs of tribes high up the Mississippi,
Who gave theirs freely, got no others for them.
This we knew was not the fault of the Lieutenant:
He was brave, and died in service of his country.

THE BUILDING OF FORT MADISON AND THE PLOT
OF THE SAUKIES TO CAPTURE IT

In Article Nine of the treaty of 'four
   A government promise was made,
As soon as a time of convenience should come,
   To establish a depot of trade.

Pursuant to this Captain Kingsley was sent[63]
   To build a trade house and a fort,
To which all the Indians in need of supplies,
   With their peltries and furs might resort.

A little way up from the rapids Des Moines,
   On a beautiful shore to the west,
They discovered a site that appeared to all eyes,
   For the purpose in view to be best.

They landed at once and with axes and spades,
   Well sharpened and wielded, soon made
From the young forest trees that were standing about,
   The walls of a fort or stockade.

The Indians learned of their coming and feared
   It might mean an infraction of peace;
So in force they came down, if perchance they might cause
   The work of the soldiers to cease.

A council was held with the Chiefs and head men,
   And the Captain so fully replied
To all of the questions the Indians could ask,
   That at last they appeared satisfied.

Black Hawk was a War Chief and did not attend
    The council, but voiced a dissent
From the views of the Chiefs and head men who were there,
    Concerning the white man's intent

While a party of soldiers were cutting down trees,
    Some Saukies were lurking about:
They quietly stole where the arms had been laid,
    And seized upon them with a shout.

The soldiers were startled, none knew what to do
    For himself or in others behalf;
But the Saukies had done all they cared to that day,
    And they gave back the guns with a laugh.

Chief Pash-e-pa-ho and Chief Quash-quam-me planned
    With Black Hawk the fort to o'erthrow,
Much as Pontiac plotted to capture the fort
    At Detroit in the days long ago.

The old Chiefs were admitted whenever they wished,
    As were others who came there to trade:
They magnified friendship, and under its guise
    A plot for the capture was laid.

With weapons concealed, many Saukies came in
    As friends might, upon a set date:
They gave entertainment with song and with dance,
    Then suddenly opened the gate.

Black Hawk and his warriors were waiting without,
    Prepared to rush in and to slay,
For the white man's fort in the red man's land
    Was marked for destruction that day;

But they saw a cannon unmasked and trained,
    And by it a soldier stand,
With a lighted match and a face like flint,
    Awaiting the word of command.

The white man's gun with the mighty voice
    Was more than they cared to fight;
So the Saukies without and the Saukies within
    Fell over each other in flight.

The few who remained were quickly searched
    And their weapons to light were brought:
They freely confessed, for they felt assured
    That the whites could read their thought.[64]

It is said that an Indian maid had learned
    Of the plot to destroy the fort,
And had come to her soldier lover there
    Bringing a full report.

The Attack of Winnebagoes and Sauks Upon Fort Madison

The Shawnee Prophet sent his men[65]
    Wherever friends might be,
Requesting them at once to join
    The great conspiracy.

One came to Saukenauk and said,
    "Do as we wish you to:
Join with us, or Americans
    Will take this town from you."

The Saukies were not much impressed,
    And so they said him nay:[66]
The messenger with downcast face
    Went on his homeward way.

The Winnebagoes did respond,
    And sent a fighting band
To join the Shawnee Prophet's force,
    Contending for their land.

Upon a famous battle field
    It was their lot to meet
With William Henry Harrison,
    Who compassed their defeat.[67]

The Winnebagoes could not take
    Straight vengeance for their dead,
And they resolved to go against
    Fort Madison instead.

The Saukies under Black Hawk joined
    With them in this attack,
With full conviction that the fort
    Would fall ere they came back.

At night they came and hid themselves,
    For it was their surmise,
That all the soldier's would march out
    Each morn for exercise.

They thought at that time they would shoot
    And, rushing to the gate,
Would thus prevent return of those,
    Who might be spared by fate.

But two or three came out, and when
    One of these men was slain,
The soldiers seemed to think it wise
    Within walls to remain.

Assault and siege were carried on
    For three or four full days:
The Indians with flaming shots
    Enkindled many a blaze.

The soldiers using all their wits,
    As such a time requires,
With rifle barrel syringes
    Put out the glowing fires,

While cannon roared and rifles rang
  Their messages each day,
Until the Indians owned defeat
  And sadly went away.

Some Statements by Black Hawk

Soon after we came back we learned
  That there was war in sight:
The British and Americans
  Were almost sure to fight.

The British agent, Dixon, held
  Long talks with diff'rent tribes:
He gave them many presents, too,
  Not to be classed as bribes.

I had not yet made up my mind:
  A British aid to be
Or, as an Indian, to abide
  In strict neutrality.

I did not know a reason why
  I needed long to wait;
For in Americans who'd come
  I'd found not one good trait.

They always made fair promises,
  But left them unfulfilled:
The British people made but few,
  But always were well willed.

    . . . . . .

One of our people killed a man,
  Somewhere up river way:
The British captured him and said,
  He must be shot next day.

He asked to be released that night
  That he might go and see,
Where in the woods they were encamped,
  His wife and family.

Their meeting and their parting there
  I can not so describe,
That pale faced men can understand,
  Not of our race and tribe.

In all relations they sustain
  With family and kin,
They're governed by a set of rules,
  We by the heart within.

He bade them all a fond farewell,
  Then hurried to the spot
Where soldiers were awaiting him,
  And stood up to be shot.

I visited the stricken ones
  And hunted for them there,
Until their relatives could come
  And take them in their care.

        .   .   .   .   .

O, why did the Great Spirit send
  The whites with poison breath,
To drive us from our homes and lands
  And bring disease and death?

They should have stayed beyond the sea
  In their allotted place,
And left forever this fair land
  To its own native race.

Since my late visit to the whites
  My mem'ry is not good:
I may not get all that I say
  In order as I should.

There's still a buzzing in my ears:
  It must be the effect
Of city noise, but I will do
  My best to be correct.

XI.   THE SAUKS AND THE WAR OF EIGHTEEN HUNDRED TWELVE

The American Effort to Pacify the Indians

WHEN it was fully understood
   That with the British war must be
Fought out in order to maintain
   The nation's rights upon the sea,

The Government, directed by
   The wise and gentle Madison,
Called Indian Chiefs from western tribes
   To come at once to Washington.

A council there was held, and they
   Were asked to quietly refrain
From joining in the white man's war,
   And on their own lands to remain.

They were informed that they would be
   Supplied with goods, by traders sent
To points conveniently arranged
   By action of the Government.

The Saukie Chieftains, coming home,
   In full detail the story told
Of this request for neutral peace
   Put forth to men warlike and bold.

They said they had been treated well,
   And told that at Fort Madison
There were sufficient stores of goods
   To meet the needs of every one.

A credit would be given them
  On what they each might need of these,
That they might be prepared to hunt
  And thus support their families.

With this arrangement all were pleased:
  They gave endorsement and applause:
The warriors chose the path of peace,
  And very happy were the squaws.

They soon made start, and merrily
  Down stream they took their way
With spirits high they reached the fort
  The morning of the foll'wing day.

There they were kindly welcomed by
  The Captain and his soldier band,
And by the trader, who seemed glad
  To give to each a friendly hand.

He said he had a store of goods
  Sufficient to all needs supply,
And though he could no credit give
  All who could pay might come and buy.

The Indians were thunderstruck.
  The clouds made dark a joyful day:
They could not hunt without supplies,
  And for supplies they could not pay.

In vain they urged the promise made
  Their Chieftains by the President.
The trader and the Captain said
  To them no message had been sent.

Not knowing what was left to do,
  In sadness and in discontent,
The Indians went to their camp,
  And there a sleepless night they

A British Invitation to Join in the War

'Tis often dark before the dawn.
When curtains of the day were drawn
Aside, the early morning gleam
Revealed a boatman on the stream,—
A messenger he proved to be
Sent by the trader, La Gutrie,
To tell them all the gladsome news
Of goods he'd brought for them to use,
And presents and a keg of rum,
And urge them with all speed to come
To Rocky Island, there to see
How good to them he wished to be.

Like fire leaping through dry grass,
The glorious news was quick to pass
Throughout the camp, and soon canoes
Shot up the stream for none would lose
A moment in his haste to meet
This man who could their joys complete.

The flashing paddles, swung with might
For many hours, brought them in sight
Of La Gutrie's white tents and boats:
Wild yells of joy burst from their throats,
They shot their guns, their drums they beat,
In mad delight their friend to greet.

An answering volley from the isle
Rang in their happy ears, the while
The British flag before their eyes
Flung out its folds beneath the skies,
That could not be more fair and blue
Than British hearts were kind and true.

The trader, standing on the sands,
Gave welcome to the Saukie bands.
They smoked the pipe, and then he said:
"I come to you in Dixon's stead,[69]
To say the British are your friends,
Who will stand by you to far ends.

"Here are the presents he has sent,
His love for you to represent;
Here is a silken flag to wave
Above each warrior true and brave;
And, that no Saukie may be glum,
Here also is a keg of rum.
Go and enjoy yourselves to-day:
To-morrow I'll have more to say."

Enjoy themselves?　Full well they knew
How at that time that thing to do.
The night before they'd sat in gloom,
But sadness now had given room,
And wild hilarity had come,—
"Yoho! yoho! and a keg of rum!"
The celebration did not lag
That day around the British flag.

Next day the Saukies asked to take
The traders goods, and said they'd make
Return in full for every thing,
With furs and peltries in the spring.

He readily gave his consent,
And to the boats the Indians went
In haste their purchase to divide.
The trader drew Black Hawk aside
To tell the thing he had to say,
That Dixon now was at Green Bay
With arms and ammunition for
All Indians who would go to war.

Black Hawk in turn the story told,
And soon two hundred were enrolled,
All glad to take the British part,
And anxious only for the start.

Arriving at Green Bay they found
A large encampment on the ground,
Of Ottawas and Kickapoos
And Winnebagoes, one might choose.
They were well armed and clothed and fed,
And waited only to be led
Forth to the conflict, there to stand
As soldiers for their friends and land.

Black Hawk at Green Bay

The Black Hawk, being summoned, went
To meet with Dixon in his tent,
   And other white men who were there:
They greeted him in kindly ways,
With many words they spoke his praise,
   And then explained their plans with care.

The Colonel said: "You brought to me
A letter from our friend, Gutrie.
   He tells us what has taken place.
You now must hold us by the hand,
And in the coming war must stand
   For us and for the Indian race.

"The British father knows about
The Long Knives' plan to drive you out
   From your own hunting grounds and fires;
And he has sent brave men to fight,
As well they should for what is right,
   And bring to nought all their desires.

"My good friend, General Black Hawk, you
Whom we all know as brave and true,
      Are now appointed to command
The red men, that from here we send
The rights of Britain to defend,
      And for themselves to keep their land."

Then spoke the Black Hawk: "I must say
All is not well with me to-day.
      Your planning does not suit my will.
Though here are arms and clothes and food
And other things considered good,
      I'm sadly disappointed still."

But Dixon said: "Behold the flag,
Be swift to answer, do not lag,
      But think of all it represents."
Then from his heart sprang to his mouth
Black Hawk's desire: "I would go south
      And war against the settlements."

"Nay, nay," the white man cried in haste:
"I've been commanded to lay waste
      The lands that lie Saint Louis way;
But I have been a trader there,
In their home life I've had a share,
      And, Black Hawk, I must say you nay.

"I can not send brave men like you
'Gainst womanhood and childhood too.
      We should not murder innocence.
It ill becomes the warrior brave
To bring down to a bloody grave
      Weak ones, who've given no offense.

"Look to the east, there are arrayed
The soldiers with their flags displayed.
      It is for us these men to meet,

To go against them in our might,
And valiantly with them to fight
   Until we compass their defeat.

"Then when an end comes to our toil,
And we shall gather in the spoil
   Our well-wrought victory secures,
The British will restore the lands
To all the Indian tribes and bands,
   And the great valley shall be yours."

The Black Hawk listened, very grave,
Then said: " 'Tis spoken by a brave,
   And I am ready now to go."
Two days thereafter at the head
Of half a thousand braves, he led
   On to the front to meet the foe.

At the Front with the British

They passed Chicago, where the fort
   Had been abandoned by
The garrison and citizens,
   Who'd thought it best to fly.

They gave it to the Indians
   And started for Fort Wayne,
But in a short time were attacked
   And many of them slain.[70]

The place of slaughter also passed,
   The Black Hawk coolly said:
"If they had kept their promises
   They would not now be dead."

Arriving at the British camp
   He found the Indians there
With captives, and he counseled them
   To treat these men with care.

A battle soon was on in which
   Americans fought well:
The British force was driven back,
   And many of them fell.

The Saukie Chief was much surprised
   At this display of might,
For he had frequently been told
   The Yankees would not fight.

.   .   .   .   .

When Procter went against Fort Meigs,[71]
   The Black Hawk's band was sent
Communication with the Fort
   By helpers to prevent.

Two men were found attending stock:
   "Don't kill these men," he said;
So they were taken prisoners
   And sent to Camp instead.

A band of soldiers, coming down
   The wide Maumee in boats,
Disabled British batteries[72]
   And routed the red coats.

Flushed with their vict'ry they pursued
   The enemy too far;
And in their turn were overcome
   By changing tide of war.

Black Hawk upon the other side
   Desired to prove his band
And quickly crossed, but came too late
   For them to take a hand.

8

The Indians in fiendish glee
   Were killing prisoners:
Black Hawk compelled them to desist,[73]
   As his account avers.

The British stayed before the fort
   For many weary days;
But finding it impregnable
   At last the siege was raised.

The Saukie force was in the woods
   And knew not what took place,
But shared the general discontent
   With others of their race.

.   .   .   .   .   .

Three months thereafter they were led[74]
   Against Fort Stephenson;
And Dixon to the Black Hawk said:
   "It quickly will be won."

As it was small, the Indian Chief
   The same opinion held;
But by the subsequent events
   This error was dispelled.

Eight men to one were kept at bay,
   And many of them killed:
The ditch before the little fort
   Was with their bodies filled.

Again did General Proctor own
   He had sustained defeat
And, gathering in his forces made[75]
   Arrangements for retreat.

Black Hawk determined to withdraw
    Because success was bad,
And through an arduous campaign
    No plunder they had had;

So, taking with him twenty braves,
    Who cared no more to fight,
He left the British camp for home[76]
    In darkness of the night.

THE EVACUATION OF FORT MADISON

In July and August of eighteen thirteen
The plucky Fort Madison oft was the scene
Of attacks by the red men who could not abide
To see it stand fair by the great river's side.

One time and again, men on duty sent out
Were slain by the Indians lurking about;
The warriors increased and all means were employed
By which the brave garrison might be destroyed;
Provisions were scant, no relief was in sight;
And at last 'twas thought best to seek safety in flight.

A trench or a tunnel was dug all the way
From the fort to the place where the waiting boats lay;
Then down it they stole, speaking never a word
Or making a sound that quick ears might have heard;
One tarried a moment the fort to devote
To the fire, then took the last place in a boat;
And before the bright flame waked the reds with its gleam
The whites were in safety afar down the stream.

And so the red men had occasion to brag
That they had cast out the American flag,
Without any aid, by their own native force,
From the Father of Waters in his upper course.

For many long years the "Lone Chimney" stood
As a mark on the site, near the edge of the wood;
And so it was called by the boatmen who passed;
But the Indians unto the dwindling last
Said "Po-to-wo-noc," or place of the fire.
City builders who came could not fail to admire
The brave men of the past, and The West being won,
They retained the old name for fair "Fort Madison."

BLACK HAWK SPARES A WOULD-BE ASSASSIN[77]

Black Hawk had nearly reached his home
 When, stooping down to drink,
In great security and peace,
 As one would surely think,

He heard a rifle hammer strike
 Upon a faulty flint
And springing up he looked upon
 A rifle barrel's glint.

The holder was a scouting white
 Who'd followed all the way,
With direst purpose in his heart.
 The red war chief to slay.

The Black Hawk swung his rifle up
 And said: "I ought to kill
You for this murderous attempt,
 Instead of that I will

"Make you a member of the tribe,
 Adopt you as my son,
And in this western land henceforth
 Your course of life shall run."

Rejoicing that his life had not
  Paid forfeit for his crime,
The scout could only acquiesce
  And calmly bide his time.

By tedious process he was made
  An Indian next day,
And such remained for three long years
  Before he broke away.

Black Hawk's Opinion of the White Man's Mode of Fighting

Black Hawk was welcomed home
  By greatest and by least:
They took him to a lodge prepared
  And sat him down to feast.

When he had eaten well,
  He looked on every one
And gave to them a full account
  Of what he'd seen and done.

"The white men do not fight
  As Indians do," said he,
"By seeking to protect themselves
  And kill the enemy.

"But boldly they march out
  In broad and open light,
Regardless of their warriors' lives,
  And carry on the fight.

"The battle being o'er,
  As though naught had occurred
They go to camp and feast and drink
  And no lament is heard.

"Each party then writes down
  The great things it has done:
It never counts but half its dead,
  But claims a vict'ry won.

"With us they could not lead,
  They pay a price too dear:
Those Chiefs might paddle a canoe,
  But are not fit to steer.

"The white men fight like braves,
  It can not be denied:
Americans are better shots
  But not so well supplied."

PROVIDING FOR THE FAMILIES OF THE BRITISH BAND

Black Hawk's Statement

I was told by the village Chief
  That when I and my band had gone
To fight at the front for the British cause,
  There were others who followed on.

The fighting men left were but few
  And if there had been an attack
By American soldiers, they would have been
  Unable to drive them back.

The women and children and old
  Of the British band were there;
And with them those that they had of their own
  Were under their watch and care.

A council was held to decide
  The thing that was best to be done,
To provide for the needs of the weak of the tribe
  And any great dangers to shun.

'Twas agreed that these people should go,
    And all others who might desire,
And place themselves in American care
    By the great Saint Louis fire.

By the white Chief stationed there
    They were welcomed with open hand,
And on the Missouri were given a home,
    As the peace, or the Quash-quam-me band.

So while with the British our bands
    Were doing their valorous deeds,
By Americans their friends were supplied
    With the things that suited their needs.

KEOKUK MADE WAR CHIEF

So many Indians had become allies
Of Britain, that it was considered wise
To strike the hostile ones wherever found,
Attack their towns and burn them to the ground.

Peoria was thus destroyed, and fear[78]
Came on the Sauks, that there would soon appear
Americans their village to lay waste:
The Chiefs convened a council in great haste.

There seemed to be one voice, and that to say:
"We must forsake our town and go away
Beyond the Mississippi's rolling tide,
And there from these oncoming forces hide."

Young Keokuk, a Chief but fourth in grade,
As was his place, without the council stayed;
But, learning of their act, was quick to seek
A chance before them to appear and speak:

"With sorrow I have learned that you decide
To leave this place and seek the other side
Because you think Americans may come.
Would you in haste forsake our village home,
Give way so quickly to unworthy fears
And fly before an enemy appears?
Would you leave all, e'en to our fathers' graves,
Without defending them as should true braves?
Give me your warriors. I'll the village keep
Against the foe, while you in safety sleep."

The council gave consent and he was made
The War Chief. Soon his plans were laid:
He marshaled warriors, sent out trusty spies
And proved himself not only brave, but wise.

He led a party, scouting all around,
But nowhere could an enemy be found.
Upon his vigilance the tribe relied:
They dwelt in safety, and were satisfied.

THE BATTLE OF CAMPBELL'S ISLAND[79]

The old fort at Prairie du Chien was held
By the British. Americans wished them expelled.
Governor Clark went up from Saint Louis in boats[80]
With a troop, and was glad to find the red coats
Had abandoned the place and gone off to Green Bay.
The Governor's force without any delay
Put up a new fort with the hope to remain
And prestige with the Indian tribes to regain.

The work well begun, the Governor came back
To provide reinforcements against an attack.
Three troop boats went up, well provisioned and big,
Commanded by Campbell and Rector and Rigg,
While contractor and suttler in little boats went
As a part of the party by common consent.

They stopped with the Saukies and felt no alarm,
For in council the Black Hawk told them that no harm
Should be done them.   They stayed a full day,
But when the wind freshened they started away.

Next morning, above the Rock Island, a gale
Struck the boats and compelled them to shorten their sail.
One craft, that of Campbell, was forced on the isle
That now bears his name.   There they tarried awhile
Expecting that soon the high wind would be o'er:
Meantime they prepared to break fast on the shore.

Down below, a great change in the Sauks had been wrought:
The British had come to their camp, and had brought
Six kegs of good powder, requesting them for
Their further assistance in brave deeds of war.

Black Hawk was responsive, and soon with his band
He had gone in pursuit, making way on the land.
His warriors were swift, and as forward they sped
Their gallant commander most naively said:

"If indeed, as I think, the Great Spirit has willed
That a boat shall be taken and people be killed,
A way to put them in our pow'r 'll be found:
This wind is his breath,— it will blow them aground."

A stealthy approach by the Saukies was made.
Through the trees and the brush, ever keeping in shade,
They drew near to the boat, then together they fired
And saw the result that so much they desired.
The sentries fell dead, but the others rushed back
To the boats and prepared to resist the attack.

The battle was hot, though the shots from the boat
Had little effect that the white men could note.
One after another an arrow of flame
From the bow of Black Hawk to the doomed vessel came:
All harmless they fell excepting the last,
Which fired the sail at the foot of the mast.

Just then the brave Rector with skill caused his boat
Down the stream to the side of brave Campbell's to float,
Transferred the survivors and drifted away
With his salvage of life from that deadly affray.

The boat of brave Rigg had found anchor below,
And now was attacked by the fierce Saukie foe.
No answer they made till the Indians came nigher,
When into their ranks they poured a hot fire,
Then loosing their vessel they drifted away
With their record of death on that terrible day.

The Indians' desire for booty was strong,
And to put out the fire did not take very long.
Just then a small skiff up the river was seen
An express, so they thought, from the Prairie du Chien:
British colors they raised to induce them to land;
But they seemed not to care for a pro-British band,
For quickly they turned and up-river they went,
While toward them the Sauks a few harmless shots sent.

In the boat there were stores of arms, clothing and food:
The Indians took over what they thought was good.
Some barrels of whiskey were standing about:
Black Hawk broke the heads and the liquor poured out.
He also threw over some drugs, for he said,
The Doctors used them to make sick people dead.

After scalping their foes and interring their friends
They went down to the place were the rocky isle ends
And with great rejoicing their trophies they bore
To the Foxes fair village not far from the shore:
There they set the old flag of the British awave
And danced o'er the scalps that the Great Spirit gave.

THE BRITISH CAPTURE FORT SHELBY AND BRING CANNON TO THE SAUKS

On July seventeenth, eighteen hundred fourteen
The British came back to the Prairie du Chien,
And there by the help of their Indian allies
Besieged the new fort, which they sought as a prize.

In four days it surrendered. The Governor Clark,
An American boat, was made a fair mark,
But escaped to bear down the sad news of defeat.
At the head of the rapids she happened to meet
With the boats of contractor and suttler, who came
With the Campbell boats even then losing the game.

Captain Yeager sent down a small skiff. It returned
With the news that one boat had been captured and burned,
And the others confessing defeat for the day,
Had loosed from their moorings and fallen away,
While the Indians, victorious, were still on the spot
And had cut the waves near them with many a shot.

The Captain delayed for a time, but at last
Raised anchor, went down the swift rapids and passed
The Fox village. The Indians raised an alarm
And followed, but could not do them any harm:
So down to Saint Louis they went to report
Brave Campbell's defeat and the loss of the fort.

When all the American boats had gone down,
A British boat came to the Foxes fair town.
They said they had captured the fort and had come
To bring greetings, big guns and a fine keg of rum.
With their Indian allies they feasted and drank
And joined in the dance round the scalps, on the bank
Then they showed how the guns should be mounted and fired
And, leaving three gunners to man them, retired.

The Repulse of Major Zachary Taylor[81]

After Campbell's defeat the up-country was held
    By the British and their allies:
Major Taylor with four hundred soldiers was sent
    "The treacherous Sauks" to chastise.

They found the Rock River too low for their boats,
    So up the great river they went;
But the Saukies and gunners were fully prepared
    Their further advance to prevent.

The wind blew a gale and their anchors they cast
    Near the shore of a small willow isle:
The river above and below them was filled
    With Indian canoemen the while.

It was late in the day and they put out their guards
    And waited throughout the long night,
Being sure that the Saukies would make an attack
    With the very first breaking of light.

Sure enough with the dawning a volley was fired,
    And a corporal fell to the foe:
The soldiers then charged, but the Saukies escaped
    To the large island lying below.

Captain Whiteside poured forth a warm fire from his boat,
    As they came to the island, and then
They stood ground a few moments, returning the fire,
    And succeeded in wounding two men.

Captain Rector dropped down to the island and raked
    All the shore with artillery fire:
He destroyed some canoes and compelled the brave foe
    Farther back in the woods to retire.

Just then the big guns of the British pealed forth
    War's message, from deep brazen throats:[82]
The gunners were skillful, the range they had found
    And damage was done to the boats.

Brave Taylor's first thought was to bring guns to bear
    And send back an answer in kind;
But as he was exposed and the foe was concealed,
    He further engagement declined.

The Saukies were yelling and shooting the while
    The American boats fell away:
They followed their foemen for several miles,
    But returning shots kept them at bay.

At a prairie below, Taylor halted to give
    Better care to his sore wounded men,
Make repairs to his boats and decide if 'twere wise
    To enter the conflict again.

A council of officers duly was held
    At which they were forced to confess,
That they were unable the foe to engage
    With any fair hope of success.

So down by the ruins of Fort Madison
    They went, bravely girding their loins,
To build a new fort on the high bluff across
    From the mouth of the river Des Moines.[83]

BLACK HAWK'S SNAKE STORY

We were sadly disappointed
    When the foe gave up the fight,
For we surely could have killed them
    Nearly all before the night.

We pursued them for some distance
  As they hastily withdrew,
And sent down a watchful party
  To observe what they might do.

When our scouting warriors came back,
  They brought with them this report:
That the whites their force had landed
  And begun to build a fort.

But no fort by us was wanted
  In our country, manned by whites,
To prevent our freely going
  Where we thought that we had rights.

So I went myself with warriors,
  That more fully we might see
What the purpose of the white men
  In their building plans might be.

We arrived late in the evening
  And without a fire or light,
Camped upon a bluff adjoining
  With our guards out for the night.

As I lay in deepest slumber
  Clear I heard the Spirit speak:
"In the morning from the hill-top
  Go down to the flowing creek,

"There you'll see a hollow tree-stump,
  And within a bright-hued snake,
Head uplifted, pointing toward
  Unarmed foes for you to take."

In the morning, rising early
  From my earth and blanket bed,
I assembled all my warriors
  And told what the Spirit said.

Then with one brave as companion,
   I descended to the creek
And discovered stump and serpent
   That the Spirit bade me seek.

Looking where the great snake pointed
   Two War Chiefs were arm in arm,
Walking slowly and conversing
   As though they were far from harm.

To the place where men were working
   On the fort they passed, and then
Turned about, descending toward us,
   But came not so nigh again.

Had they done so they would surely
   Have gone down before our fire,
For we carried goodly rifles
   And to kill was our desire.

When at last the fort they entered
   I returned half up the hill,
But my brave had seen a sentry
   And stayed in the valley still.

From my place I saw him slowly
   Creeping toward the sentry's track:
As is common 'mong the white men,
   He was moving forth and back.

Once he stopped, intently looking
   Where my warrior lay concealed,
But by neither sound nor motion
   Was his presence there revealed.

To his beat's end came the sentry.
   As he turned to walk away,
From his place my warrior fired:
   One white man was killed that day.

At the fort was great confusion,
　　When they heard the rifle's sound:
I could see them wildly running
　　To their boats and all around.

Soon my brave and I ascended,
　　By the way that we came down,
To our fellows, and the party
　　Hurried back to Saukie-town.

MAKING THE TREATY OF PEACE

The war of eighteen hundred twelve was fought
Because Great Britain arrogantly sought
To exercise her will as she might please,
Impress to service sailors on the seas,
Ignore the law of nations and blockade
Ports as she wished, destroying neutral trade.

Upon the sea, where Britain boasted sway,
America more often won the day;
While on the land, defeat and victory
In even balance ever seemed to be.

The Emperor of Russia, as a friend
Of both contestants, offered help to end
The wasting war, and bring about a peace
That through the years to come should never cease.

America agreed, her shield was bright,
And she contended only for the right;
But Britain did not, knowing her demand
Before impartial judgment could not stand.
Long she delayed, but finally proposed
Direct discussion that war might be closed.
Before the envoys met, Napoleon
To Elba's isle in sad defeat had gone,
And many British veterans had been sent
Across the ocean to this continent.

The British, arrogant, proposed to treat
As with a nation that had met defeat.
Of points at issue when the war begun
They would not yield, they said, a single one;
While for themselves and for the Indian bands
They would require water rights and lands.
In other words: the Northwest, as a prize
Once lost, must be restored to her allies;
And great concessions to themselves must be[84]
Confirmed as natural rights of victory.
This they presented as *sine qua non*.
It must be yielded if debate went on.

America replied that she had bought
Most dearly all the things for which she'd fought:
Of what she thus had well secured and paid,
She did not care that mention should be made.
She yielded nothing, this they all must know;
And she insisted on the *statu quo*.
The *statu quo* it was to all intents,
And thus we close our sketch of these events.

XII. FROM THE WAR OF EIGHTEEN TWELVE TO THE ENFORCEMENT OF THE TREATY OF EIGHTEEN FOUR

TERMS OF THE TREATY REGARDING THE INDIANS

BY the treaty each nation was bound to restore
   To its Indians the rights that had been theirs before,[85]
On condition that they from all warfare should cease
And henceforth with the white men continue at peace.

SOME POST-WAR RAIDS

The British band of the Sauks
   Were flushed with their victories,
And they were displeased that the war should close
   In the very face of these.

Encouraged by Englishmen,
   Who were their advisers and aids,
For many long months they carried on
   A series of petty raids.[86]

White people were cruelly slain,
   Or captured and carried away;
Many horses were stolen, and fear of red men
   Throughout the whole region had sway.

.   .   .   .   .   .

Black Hawk with about forty braves
   Went down to where Fort Howard stood,
With design to inflict on the people near by
   Such harm as he thought that he should[87]

When they drew their canoes to the land
     They fell in with a party of five:
Three were slaughtered and scalped, one received a death
          wound,
     But the fifth man escaped them alive.

The soldiers came forth from the fort
     And a very sharp battle was fought:
The Saukies were worsted and, fleeing away,
     In a sink-hole for refuge they sought.

The whites made a breastwork on wheels
     And, pushing it down to the brink,
They exchanged a few shots with the Indian foe,
     Concealed in the depths of the sink.

Darkness coming, the soldiers withdrew:
     The Saukies made haste to come out
And depart with their wounded, leaving the slain
     On the battlefield lying about.[88]

*   *   *   *   *   *

Robert Ramsey of County Saint Charles
     Had a wife and children three,
And a little home, all as dear to his heart
     As yours to you may be.

They were near to the house in the yard,
     At the close of a happy day:
The wife and mother was milking the cow,
     And the children were at play.

The man with his wooden leg
     Was standing beside his wife:
About them there was the calm of peace,
     With never a thought of strife.

A rifle shot rang out,
    And the crippled husband bore,
As best he was able, his wounded wife
    To the humble cabin door.

He tenderly laid her down,
    And turned to his children's aid;
But another bullet laid him low,
    Ere scarcely a step he had made.

The Indians came with a rush:
    They slaughtered the children three,
And horribly mangled their tender forms,—
    A terrible sight to see.

．　．　．　．　．　．

A young man and his sister had started away
To the home of a neighbor to visit one day,
When the youth was struck down by an Indian shot
And the maiden was rudely borne off from the spot.

Sorely wounded the youth crawled back to the farm,
Told what had occurred, and soon the alarm
Went out o'er the prairies, till from far and wide
Came well-mounted settlers determined to ride

Till they rescued the maiden or traced to their lair
Her captors, and made them take punishment there.
Their horses were fleet, and they followed the track
Till they came on the Indians, and took the girl back.

Treaties of Peace and Friendship

It was not the desire of the Government
To be harsh; but it felt that it must prevent
These murderous raids, and without more ado

It called the head men down to Portage des Sioux,
A council to hold and a treaty to make
That should settle all issues that might be at stake.

The Peace, the Missouri or Quashquamme band,
With a full delegation was promptly at hand,
As also the Foxes, who'd given small aid
To the British in war or the Saukies in raid.

The treaty of eighteen and four was reviewed
And in separate treaties its terms were renewed,[89]
With further provisions for friendship and peace
That, through all the years, it was hoped would not cease.

. . . . . .

But a peace with the peaceful, though good in its way,
Was not of much moment while Black Hawk held sway
O'er an arrogant band, that had twice put to rout
Brave soldiers the nation in pride had sent out.

The issue was joined: it was well understood
That the Sauks would be wise to seek peace while they
        could,
Or Jackson would come, who, within a few weeks,
Had slain in the South more than ten hundred Creeks.[90]

The Foxes asked Black Hawk a treaty to make
Lest American forces should war undertake:
Other Indians urged, and the trader, Gutrie,
Said he knew this the wish of the British to be.[91]

But Black Hawk would not yield till the following May,
When with Chiefs and head men he went Saint Louis way.
The council was hot, for the whites made it plain
That the reds must repent if they wished to obtain
Forgiveness for injuries, grievous and sore,
And retain all the rights that had been theirs before.

The treaty of 'four was considered again,
Reaffirmed and made part of the new one, and then,
All things having been on a paper writ down,
It was signed by both parties in Saint Louis town.[92]

THE BUILDING OF FORT ARMSTRONG

The Government had felt the Saukies' power,
And did not wish that any evil hour
Might find it with an insufficient force
Should they again pursue a warlike course:
Besides it hoped the Indian trade to gain
For its own people through its broad domain.

At Rocky Island's foot upon a ledge,
That rises sharply from the water's edge,
It built Fort Armstrong, square four hundred feet,
With ports and towers and magazine complete,
As long as need should be to firmly stand
Within the very heart of Saukie-land.

The work was done and well done by a band
Of soldiers under General Smith's command.
'Twas on the twelfth of May, eighteen sixteen,
That they appeared in force upon the scene.
Direction of affairs was given o'er
To Colonel Lawrence: well his part he bore,
And in due time the fort desired was there,
Old glory waving o'er it on the air.

The Indians watched with sullen discontent,
And wondered much what such proceeding meant.
A treaty had been signed: what was it for,
If white men could at once prepare for war?
Besides the island was a sacred place,—
A spirit dwelt there, (honored by their race,)
With great white wings: they could not think it right
That it thus rudely should be put to flight.

REBUILT BLOCK HOUSE ON THE SITE OF THE SOUTH ANGLE OF
FORT ARMSTRONG

DAVENPORT HOUSE AS RESTORED, ON THE ISLAND OF ROCK ISLAND   *i*

George Davenport

Antoine LeClaire

John W. Spencer

John Dixon

But these white men were wise: in kindly way
They sought the reds' resentment to allay,
And as the days went by they slowly gained
Their confidence, which was for years retained.

Among the men who came to build the fort,
The Commissary, Colonel Davenport,[93]
Decided to engage in Indian trade,
And near at hand a proper house was made.

An Englishman by birth, this land he'd sought
And in the war of eighteen twelve had fought,
With Scott up north and Jackson in the south,
High honors gaining at the cannon's mouth.

Another man of equal weight and worth,
Much loved, was French and Indian by birth:
In all relations he was just and fair,
The good interpreter, Antoine LeClaire.[94]

An Indian Agent to the fort was sent
To keep the tribes in touch with Government,
Develop friendship, peaceful times insure,
And all their fruits to reds and whites insure.

BLACK HAWK TELLS OF HIS MOURNING FOR HIS CHILDREN

When spring-time came my eldest son,
 Who was my joy and pride
And had arrived at manhood's years,
 Was taken sick and died.

Soon after this my little girl,
 Affectionate and mild,
Was taken to the spirit land,—
 She was my youngest child.

The stroke was hard.   In my distress
    I could not bear the sound
Of village life, and built my lodge
    Upon a lonely mound.

About it I put up a fence
    And planted corn and beans:
There with my family I lived
    Apart from festive scenes.

I gave away all I possessed,
    And in my grief and woe
I only wore a piece of skin
    Stripped from the buffalo.

I blacked my face, and was indeed
    In most pathetic plight:
My food was boiled corn,—sparingly
    I ate of it at night.

Through twenty-four long, weary moons
    I magnified my grief
Until the Spirit pitied me
    And came to my relief.

BLACK HAWK AND OTHER INDIANS VISIT THE BRITISH AT DRUMMOND'S ISLAND JULY 12TH, 1821

Black Hawk Makes an Address

My Father, I am not able to speak:
    I may say what I ought not to say.
My Father, I may bring words of reproach:
    Very few have come with me to-day.

Since I started from home, all the way as I came
    One thought in my mind there has been:
That I was approaching my Great Father's fire,
    Where his soldiers would cover my skin.

Because of the barriers I could not cross
  For three years, I have cause to believe
That now I have come, from my Father's great store
  Double portion I'll surely receive.

Americans, Father, encompass us round,
  But with them we are ready to meet.
So seldom we come, we hope you'll give more
  Than to Indians that yearly you greet.

My Father we look for your charity now,
  We hope that good gifts you will make:
Our wives and our children expect to be warmed
  By the clothes that to them we shall take.

This wampum declares for a broad, open way
  From our homes to our Great Father's fire:
Your counsels we always have fully obeyed,
  And to do so henceforth we desire.

The Indians have never attempted to bar
  Our way to our Great Father's side;
But white men around us, who seem to be strong,
  Would prefer that at home we abide.

Answer of Lieutenant Colonel William McKay[95]
British Indian Superintendent

My children, I have heard what you have said:
Through open ears your words have reached my head.
When last you came, whatever you believed,
A larger share of bounty you received
Than other Indians; and you then were told
That Amherstburg your future gifts would hold.
You seemed to be displeased and wanted more.
Again I treat you well, but as before
You are dissatisfied. Now go your way,
But bear in mind that in a future day

Your gifts will be at Amherstburg, and there,
If bounty you would have, you must repair.
I've done my best to please you here to-day,
But it would seem my work is thrown away.
You may go home. I do not wish to see
Unhappy children coming after me.

About the stopped up roadway, as you say,
I have not heard of it until to-day,
Nor do I know of steps to that effect,
Or any action of that kind expect.
If you behave yourselves, as I have said,
I do not think that you have aught to dread.
Good counsel take, and nothing will transpire
To keep you back from your Great Father's fire.

THE FINAL CONFLICT BETWEEN THE SAUKS AND THE IOWAS[96]

May 1st, 1823

The Iowa tribe was more mild
    And more chaste in social relations
Than were the surrounding tribes,
    Or so-called Indian nations.

They could not successfully stand
    'Gainst invasions and dread depredations
By the warlike Saukies and Sioux,
    And were forced to frequent migrations.

In an action at Iowaville
    The Saukies in one dreadful hour
Destroyed a large part of the tribe
    And forever deprived them of power.

Unarmed, the warriors and braves,
    Not thinking of warfare or pillage,

Were engaged in a program of sports
    In the bottom, two miles from the village.

The height of excitement was reached
    In a very close race of their horses:
Meanwhile in a forest near by
    The Saukies had gathered their forces.

They were led by Chief Pash-e-pa-ho,
    And were marshaled in two strong divisions:
Under Black Hawk a third had been sent
    To the village to do there occisions.

As the horses were nearing the goal
    The terrible war whoop was sounded,
And forth from the forest, well armed,
    A host of the Saukie braves bounded.

The Iowas, startled and dazed,
    Made a dash for their arms at the village,
But to find, as they neared, 'twas ablaze,
    A wild scene of warfare and pillage.

The shrieks of their children and wives
    With the yells of the Saukies were blended,
As the tomahawk gleamed in the light
    And on the defenseless descended.

Though few were the arms they could find,
    They rushed to their loved ones' assistance,
And seizing on clubs and on stones,
    They made a most desp'rate resistance.

But the odds were too great for their strength,
    And warriors, children and women,
In bloody destruction by scores,
    When down 'neath the arms of the foemen.

A remnant from slaughter was spared;
    But all power from them had been riven,
And they ceased to hold much of the state
    To which their fair name has been given.

Various Treaties

In the year twenty-two a new treaty was made
With the Sacs and the Foxes, and money was paid
To release the U. S. from maintaining a store
According to treaty of eighteen and four.
'Twas a technical matter, for traders at hand
Were dealing directly with each Indian band.

. . . . . .

In August, eighteen twenty-four
    These tribes made a treaty again:
This time with Commissioner Clarke,
    Through chosen and deputized men.

By its terms they sold and quit-claimed
    All their rights in Missouri to lands,
For ten years annuities pledged
    And monies or goods in their hands.

. . . . . .

The tribes of the up-river country
    Had a strong inclination to fight;
And every occasion of conflict
    Was welcomed by them with delight.

The Government called them in council
    In the year twenty-five at "du Chien,"
With the hope that the evils of warfare
    By them as they were might be seen.

There were various tribes represented:
　　The Sacs and the Foxes, the Sioux,
The Iowas, wild Winnebagoes,
　　Menominees,—Chippewas, too.

Pottawatomies came in small numbers,
　　And Ottawas answered as well:
All assembled, secure in their virtues,
　　The vices of others to tell.

After fully discussing the matter
　　They consented their warfare to cease;
And the Government's right they conceded
　　To act as an umpire of peace.

Lines were drawn to rectify bound'ries
　　And sessions of lands were confirmed:
A council of far-reaching import,
　　This gath'ring of nations was termed.

The results were set forth in a treaty
　　That bound the U. S. and each tribe,
To which, when the work was completed,
　　All present were glad to subscribe.

.　.　.　.　.　.

Nothwithstanding the pact of eighteen twenty-five
The Sioux with the Saukies continued to strive;
So in eighteen and thirty a treaty was made,
By which to the Government each tribe conveyed
A strip next the boundary twenty miles wide,
Over which no war party of Indians should ride.

The Winnebago "War"

In the year twenty-seven a Sioux band
　　Without an assignable cause,
Not far from the walls of Fort Snelling,
　　Took the lives of some brave Chippewas.

Four Sioux, who were captured by soldiers,
　Were turned to their Chippewa foes,
Who gave to each one thirty paces
　And in turn brought their lives to a close.

The Sioux tribe, incensed and revengeful,
　But fearing the Government's power,
Sought to bring the wild Winnebagoes
　To their aid in this evil hour.

So they told them the men who were captured
　Were all Winnebagoes, and rights
Could only be saved for their nation
　By killing a number of whites.

Red Bird and some others, in cabins
　By stealthy attack slaughtered four,
But as that only equaled the culprits
　Other means were adopted for more.

Two boats going down from Fort Snelling
　Were attacked by a party of braves:
Four white men were slain in the action,
　And eight Winnebagoes found graves.

Red Bird, the great Chieftain surrendered:
　He was put in a prison and died.
Seven others were soon apprehended,
　And by legal processes were tried.

Two of these were convicted and sentenced;
　But to their great joy and behoof
The others were duly acquitted,
　Because there was lack of full proof.

It was said that the Sac Chieftain, Black Hawk,
　Was one of the men who were tried
For attacking the boats on the river;
　But this has been stoutly denied.

THE ATTITUDE OF GOVERNOR EDWARDS AND GOVERNOR REYNOLDS TOWARD THE INDIANS

In the year 'twenty-six when Edwards came[97]
  Again to the Governor's chair,
He planned the removal of all the reds
  From the state while he should be there.

The northern half was a broad expanse
  Of the continent's best lands;
But the whites were few, and the Indians roamed
  As they would in scattered bands.

He urged his case with the President[98]
  And some success he gained;
But when in 'thirty he left his place
  Many red men still remained.

. . . . . .

Governor Reynolds had given adherence[99]
  To many of Edwards' plans,
And being "A Man of the People"
  This cause was safe in his hands.

XIII. ENFORCING THE TREATY OF
EIGHTEEN FOUR

IN the year 'twenty-eight Sacs and Foxes were told
That according to treaty their lands would be sold,
And they must remove to the Iowa ground
Where good village sites could be readily found.

The first one with his band to take counsel and go
Was the Chief of the Foxes, the great Wapello,
Then Keokuk stated that he would retire
Whenever the whites should see fit to require.

But Black Hawk protested, his love was so strong
For his village, moreover he thought it was wrong
For white men to take land, and he would not admit
That the treaty was valid by which they claimed it.

Colonel Davenport knew the Sac language quite well,
And with careful detail he proceeded to tell
To his friend, the Black Hawk, what the treaty contained,
And of difficult times if the Indians remained.

With kindness he urged him to do the best thing,
To select a new site and remove in the spring;
But Black Hawk it appeared had made up his mind,
And to take such advice did not seem much inclined.

The old chief asked that Keokuk seek to arrange,[100]
If he could, with the Government for an exchange
Of other choice lands for the loved village site,
In almost any way it might think to be right.

This Keokuk gladly consented to do,
And made every effort to see the thing through:
Some relief was thus brought to Black Hawk's troubled
        breast,
And he went to the hunt with a hope for the best.

But within a few months information came down
That white men had moved into the Indian town.
The Black Hawk was indignant, and hastening back
He told them to go elsewhere,—of land was no lack.

He went to the trader, who still thought it best
For him to give up and remove to the west.
Such counsel again made the old warrior hot,
And he said with some emphasis that he would not.

With the dawn of the day he again started forth
To seek the sub-agent away to the north,
Who dwelt with the bold Winnebagoes, and know
What his counsel might be.   It was this: he should go.

The Black Hawk was displeased with what white men had
        said,
And concluded to seek the advice of a red;
So he turned him about, and went hastily down
By the Rock River way to the Prophet's fair town.

Winneshiek listened gravely to all that he told[101]
And answered him thus: "If your town was not sold
The whites can not drive you away from your lands.
Tell Keokuk so, and return with your bands."

Black Hawk was delighted, and hastened away
To find out what Keokuk might have to say.
He was willing to try, and consented to bring
All the Sauks to the village again in the spring.[102]

Judge Spencer the story so fully has told[103]
Of the Saukies and settlers, our hand we withold,
Save to put it in lines that may harmonize well,
As a part of the tale we are trying to tell.

When the summer came on, Colonel Davenport went
To Washington City, that he might present
The Black Hawk's contention with fulness and care,
To his friend, who now sat in the President's chair.

10

"Old Hickory" listened until he had done,
And the Colonel had hopes that his case might be won;
But Jackson's eyes glowed with a gathering fire,
And at last he broke forth with all symptoms of ire:

"If I understand whom it is you plead for,
This is the same band that fought us in the war;
Then, By the Eternal! the thing has been willed.
They must all cross the river or they will be killed."

Then Davenport asked a few months of delay.
This Jackson conceded. "They must be away
By April the first, however," he said,
"And any who tarry may find themselves dead."

Governor Edwards was stirred by this leniency,
And on first reaction decided that he
Would take the whole matter into his hands
And forcibly oust these troublesome bands.

But on second thought he concluded to wait
Till the nation should finally join with the state
In driving the Sauks to the Iowa shore
And enforcing the treaty of eighteen and four.

Before leaving that fall for the far hunting ground
Black Hawk went to see if the trader had found
Any news that was good; but instead he was told
That the land of the village had been ordered sold.

And that when it passed from the Government's hands
It could not be home for the Indian bands:
The rights of the purchasers would be upheld,
And Indians coming there would be expelled.

The land was soon sold. Colonel Davenport bought
A large part, for being the owner he thought
Should the Nation consent that a change might be made.
Would put him in better position to aid,

The news filtered down to the camp of Black Hawk.
There was many a council and many a talk:
It was fully resolved to return in the spring,
Whatever result such action might bring.

With purpose of vengeance their bosoms were filled:
If they were expelled, those to blame should be killed.
The trader was first in the list they made out:
Since he purchased the land, he was guilty no doubt.

The Interpreter, Agent, the fort Commandant,
The great Chief at Saint Louis, who hearings should grant,
And Keokuk, too, who avoided all strife:
Each of these should account for his deeds with his life.

When April came round, from the camp every Sauk,[104]
Who wished to do so, returned with Black Hawk;
But two-thirds of them chose by the treaty to stand,
And with Keokuk went to the Iowa land.

No one at Rock Island seemed glad to receive
The Black Hawk, and the Agent told him he must leave.
This roused the old Chief, and he said he would stay,
That white men had no right to drive Indians away.

He called on Le Claire, the Interpreter, then,
But the Agent's command was repeated again,
Except that it came in the way of advice,
That Black Hawk like some others did not think was nice.

With blood that was boiling, a third call he made,
On Davenport then, and began to upbraid
Him for posing as friend of the Indian bands
And then buying up the best part of their lands.

The Colonel attended him through to the end,
Then he said: "It is true I'm the Indians' friend,
And in this I have done the best thing that I could:
Had I not bought the land there are others who would.

"If your tribe with the Government can so arrange,
I am ready and willing to make an exchange."
The Black Hawk was convinced that the trader had bought
With good will, and was not near as bad as he'd thought.

Davenport's proposition was formally made,
The Great Chief at Saint Louis consented to aid,
A council of Saukies endorsed the whole plan
And chose to present it their Chief and Head Man.

Keokuk with Le Claire to the capital went,
And was kindly received by the great President:
With all of his eloquence "Cicero" plead,
And Jackson gave heed to each word that he said;

But he would not consent that exchange should be made:
Removal already had long been delayed:
Not a Sauk had a right in that region to stay:
Forthwith they must go or be driven away.

As the summer of 'thirty wore on the Black Hawk
Called upon many men for the purpose of talk:
He said to them all that the town was not sold,
And in turn by them all was as frequently told,

That if such was the case and they lived there in peace,
All efforts to move them would finally cease.
The Chief of the British at Malden was sure
That their good behavior all rights would secure.

When he came back from Malden, his people had gone
To the far hunting ground, and he soon followed on.
He kept touch with the Prophet, and ventured to bring
All his band to the village again in the spring.[105]

He was met by the Agent, who said he must go,
And added in kindness, 'twould be better so;
For then he would find all his troubles would cease
And he could abide with his people in peace.

The Interpreter joined in the Agent's request,
And good reasons gave why such course would be best.
Black Hawk was much moved, but he'd taken his stand,
And his pledge had been made to the brave Saukie band.

He went to the trader, who spoke of distress
That would come to his women and children unless
He removed ere the soldiers with cannon should come,
Under orders to drive them away from their home.

Then the Colonel enquired what sum he would ask
To give up forever his difficult task:
Would six thousand dollars suffice him to pay
The expenses involved in his going away?

After much careful thought Black Hawk said he would take
That amount, if the Chief at Saint Louis would make
Such an offer, and then he at once would remove
From the place of his birth, and the land of his love.

By a boat that was passing a messenger went,
And an answer brought back that not even a cent
Was the National Government willing to pay,
But the soldiers would drive all the Saukies away.

Black Hawk asked the Prophet what course he should take,
And was counseled no sort of resistance to make,
But to be as indifferent as he well could,
Allowing the soldiers to do what they would.

General Gaines and his soldiers came early in June,[106]
When all nature seemed to be in perfect tune.
A council was called of the Fox and the Sac:
There was ready response,—no one seemed to hold back.

Wapello, the Head Man of the Foxes, was there
And Keokuk, Chief of the Saukies, to share
In an effort to settle this matter aright
And preserve good relations 'twixt red men and white.

Black Hawk and his band came in warlike array,
And singing their war songs they made a display.
To let it be known that they came without fear,
They raised the war whoop as the door they drew near,

And demanded that other red men go away;
But at length they consented the Chieftains might stay.
General Gaines unaffected by this martial stress,
Arose and proceeded to make an address.

He said the Great Father was sorry to find
That some of his children did not seem inclined
To abide by the treaty and move to the west,
At his oft repeated and kindly behest.

Beyond this, he said, he had nothing to tell,
Except that the President wished them all well,
And asked of them only the thing that was right,
That they leave the country and seek a new site.

Then Black Hawk replied in words forceful and bold:
"This land is our own.   It has never been sold,
And we are determined upon it to stay.
We will not give it up, and will not go away.

General Gaines was aroused by this violent talk,
And he sprang to his feet crying, "Who is Black Hawk?"
The old warrior replied, "I'm a Sac, I'm a Sac?
All my forefathers were, and they call me a Sac."

The General said that one thing they must know,
He came neither to beg nor to hire them to go,
But to see that they went, in peace or by force,—
He would give them two days to decide on their course.

The council broke up, and the old warrior then
Sought advice from the Rock River Prophet again.
He was told to send one of his squaws to the fort,
Old Mattatas' daughter, to make a report

That her father, who long was a Chief in the band,
Had never known aught of the sale of the land;
And to put forth a plea in the name of their toil,
For the rights that the women should have in the soil.

The General received her with kindness and said,
He came not to make treaties with women, instead
To enforce one that warriors had long ago made;
But if she was in need he would see she had aid.

The militia arrived, and the General led
His force 'gainst the village, but Black Hawk had fled.[107]
In a camp with his people he later was found
About eight miles below on the Iowa ground,

And was called to the fort with his warriors, where he
In a council assembled was forced to agree,
Through articles duly attested and signed
That all claim to his village he henceforth resigned,

That contention regarding the treaty should cease,
And in good faith accepting this issue of peace,
Himself and the whole British band would abide
Through all coming years on the Iowa side.

The General moved by compassion gave heed
To the Indians' condition, supplying their need
From the stores at the fort, and arranging to give
Full measures of corn by which they might live.

XIV. THE SETTLERS AND THE SAUKIES

Paraphrased from the Reminiscenses of Judge J. W. Spencer

I WAS born in old New England
And came west in eighteen-twenty,
When I was a youth of nineteen,
To Saint Louis, then a city
Of about five thousand people.
In that County lived an Uncle;
But with others he was planning
To remove to Illinois,
For the well-considered reason
That Missouri was a slave state.[108]
So I came back with a cousin
To a settlement called Bluffdale,
Near the Illinois River.
There we found among our neighbors
Some men who had been with Campbell
In the Indian engagement
On an island near Rock Island,
In our second war with Britain.

Some years later there was int'rest
In the lead mines at Galena,
And in March of twenty-seven
I went up with sev'ral others,
Coming back late in the summer.
This became so much a practice
That the settlers were called "Suckers."

Next year we removed from Bluffdale
To a place in Morgan County,
On the road that leads to Beardstown.
That fall Rinnah Wells, returning

A TAMA INDIAN WICK-I-UP

A portable winter house sometimes used as a permanent home

A TAMA INDIAN SUMMER HOUSE   *b*

A type of the Sac and Fox village home

From the lead mines at Galena,
Stopped one night with us and told us
That the Indians were leaving
Their old village near Rock Island.
It was less than one week later,
That with Louden Case, the elder,
I was on my way to find out
For myself about the matter.

Near the river we fell in with
Mr. Prince, who came from Princeville
With a load that he was hauling
For Judge Pence, who was removing
To the Saukie Indian village.
Pence was in advance. We followed
In the tracks made by his wagon,
And crossed over to the island.
There we came upon him, looking
For a place to ford the channel,
Which was deeper, to the village.
Finding one, we soon passed over.
There were several Indian dwellings:
In a large one we took shelter.
Judge Pence, early in the morning,
Started out and found another,
Which was better. It was Black Hawk's,
As was later on developed.

These rude dwellings were constructed
Out of light poles for a framework,
With elm bark for walls and roofing.
They were sixteen feet by twenty,
Sometimes wider, often longer;
And served well for summer houses.

For their winter homes, the Indians
Make of poles a rounded framework,

Which they cover o'er with matting,
Woven out of flags and rushes.
At the top there is an opening
For the smoke to find an exit.
Indians say they make small fires
And get close to them, but white men
Make great fires and stand afar off.

When we came, there were no Indians,
And it was not thought by settlers,
Or the soldiers on the island,
That they ever would come back here.
These at that time were the settlers:
Judge Pence at the Indian village;
Captain Clark and one named Haney,
Near the Mississippi River,
Opposite Rock Island Fortress;
Archie Allen and George Harlan,
Conrad Leak and Thomas Kinney,
Farther up at Rapids City.

Having chosen a location
I returned to Morgan County,
Where I made my preparation
To remove here in the spring-time.
March the first we reached Rock Island,[109]
And found temporary quarters
In a wigwam on the hillside.
That same spring came many others.
Shortly after our arrival,
To the village came two Indians.
One of them talked very loudly
Speaking in the Indian language,
Which none present could interpret.

Pointing to the Indian dwellings,
"Saukie wigeop," he shouted.
To the ground about he pointed

Crying, "Aukie, Saukie aukie."
Many times these words he uttered,
Till we knew that he was claiming
Lands and dwellings for his people.

This man proved to be the Black Hawk.
Till that time we had no knowledge
That such Chief as he existed.
He had heard where he was camping
Of the coming of the white men,
And had come with his attendant
To learn more about their purpose.

Going to his own large dwelling,
Where Judge Pence's folks were living,
He appeared to be offended.
Quickly calling their attention
To the posts that had been injured
By the action of the fire,
He informed them quite directly,
That if they must have such fires,
Then the posts must be protected.

Coming to the Indian dwelling,
Which we then were occupying,
'Tis not to be greatly wondered
That the old man was excited.

It was nearly six weeks later,
In the latter part of April,
That he came back with his people.
By that time Judge Pence was living
In his own well-built log cabin,
In the limits of the village.

Much displeased were all the Indians
At the presence of the white men;
And one day about two hundred

Of the young men of the village,
Mounted on their swiftest ponies,
Rode around Judge Pence's cabin
Several times in threatening manner.

Mrs. Prince, alone with children,
Was alarmed, and sent the eldest
To the fort to ask protection.
Captain Nelson, the Commander,
Sent Le Claire to tell the Indians
They must be on good behavior
Or be visited by soldiers.

After that they were more quiet
And we got along together
Pretty well, save for some trouble
That they had with Wells and Vandruff.

All the Indian agriculture
Was conducted by the women,
With sometimes a slight assistance
Given by the boys and old men.

Only once, as I remember,
Did I see a young man working
In the field, and he was building
One of their weak Indian fences,
Sticking stakes and tying thereto
Little poles to serve as barriers.

All they used in cultivating
Was the hoe, and corn and squashes
With fine beans and luscious melons
Were the only crops attempted.

Ere our Indians leave in autumn,
For their winter hunting quarters,
They make caches of provisions.

DESCENDANTS OF BLACK HAWK
Overlooking Rock Island and Davenport

INDIAN CORNFIELD IN SOUTH ROCK ISLAND TOWNSHIP
Showing hills made by the squaws many years ago

b

This is commonly their method:
Cutting from the sod a circle
One foot and a half across it,
They dig downward five or six feet,
All the while the hole enlarging.
Then they line the sides and bottom
With elm bark, and store their produce,
Corn and beans, dried corn and squashes,
Sometimes also small crab apples,
In strong sacks of their own making.
Over all they put more elm bark
And tamp down the earth upon it.
Then with care the sod replacing
And the surplus dirt removing,
They leave, hoping when they come back
They will find there their provisions.

Very soon the Winnebagoes,
And quite often other Indians,
With their muskrat spears come searching,
Probing in the ground and searching,
For the caches of the Saukies.
When they find them, they despoil them.
This is robbery for certain,
But I know of no disturbance
'Twixt the tribes resulting from it.
In the spring time, when our Indians
Come back from their winter hunting,
Those whose caches have been broken
Are supplied from small collections
That are made throughout the village.

All our Indians were governed
By their Civil Chiefs and War Chiefs.
'Twas the duty of the Peace Chiefs
To adjust all difficulties
'Twixt their tribe and other Indians,

Also 'twixt them and the white men.
Never did the War Chiefs meddle
With the business of the village,
Though in times of serious trouble
Peace and War Chiefs worked together.

Of the War Chiefs, two were leaders:
They were Keokuk and Black Hawk,
Heads of the opposing parties,
The American and British.

Colonel Davenport informed me
That it had become a practice
For our British band of Indians,
As of others in the north west,
Frequently to visit Malden,
There to pay court to the English.[110]

In large numbers they would gather
Near Detroit, this side the river,
There to wait a day appointed
For each tribe to be called over
And be given entertainment.
They were met with bands of music
And escorted to the fortress,
Where a feast for them was waiting
And a great deal was provided
For their pleasure and amusement.

Keokuk we felt was friendly,
And one day we called upon him,
Offering to plow his cornfield.
Our proposal was accepted,
And at once the work proceeded.
Frequently he came out to us,
Treating us to sweetened water,
Which the Indians considered
As indeed a very nice drink.

When the corn was nearly knee high,
Keokuk called all the settlers
And proposed to put up cattle
In the night-time, for the fences
Of the Indians would not stop them.
Indians would watch in day-time,
And no cattle should be injured.
All but Rinnah Wells consented:
He thought it was too much trouble.

When the corn reached roasting stages,
One night Mr. Well's cattle
Ate the crop of sev'ral Indians.
On the next night when the cattle
Came back for another helping,
Very carefully the Indians
Turned them into his own cornfields.
After that he kept them yarded.

Very well I knew the Black Hawk,
Living near him all one summer.
He was medium in stature,
And his age I judge was sixty.
As a neighbor he was quiet,
Peaceable and kindly-hearted.
Very strong was he for temperance.
One day with some braves to help him
He called on the whiskey-seller,
Rolled out of the door his barrels,
With his hatchet knocked the heads in,
Thus destroying all the liquor.
For this he was called to answer
By the Agent, who informed him
Such things would not be permitted.

When he left the council chamber,
To Le Claire I heard the Black Hawk
Say, that he would give up effort

To prevent his men from drinking,
For it got him into trouble.
He himself would do no drinking
And would be found wearing wampum;
If the young men kept on drinking
They could only dress in swansdown.

At the village poles were standing,
Some of which were bearing branches.
On these poles they hung their trophies,
And around them held their dances.
If in raid, foray or battle
They have lost some of their number,
On return they do no dancing.

In the first year that I lived here,
Forty of our Saukie Indians
Swam the river in the night-time,
Broke into a Sioux encampment
Of about one hundred lodges,
And with knives killed fifteen warriors,
Losing two men in the struggle.
Coming back they held no dances,
But instead they blacked their faces,
Mourning for their lost companions.

This same season three brave warriors,
Scouting near the great Missouri,
Saw an Indian on the prairie.
Omaha he was they felt sure.
Quickly climbing to the branches
Of a low and bushy alder,
Like a deer one of them bleated.
When the Omaha approached them,
From their hiding-place they shot him,
And bore home in glorious triumph
Scalp-lock, gun and horse's bridle.

This time there was great rejoicing,
And a dance was quickly planned for.
Round the poles the three brave warriors
And the squaws to them related,
Bearing high the gory scalp-lock,
Leaped and bounded, loudly boasting.

Round about young men were standing,
Gaily painted and observing.
One old man was loudly beating
On a rude drum, made by stretching
On a keg a piece of rawhide.
Other old men sang so loudly
That in stillness of the night-time
Sev'ral miles their voices carried.
Now and then the dance subsided,
And some old men, stepping forward,
Told in loud and boastful accents
Of a great exploit in battle.
All the Indians then shouted,
And again the dance proceeded.
Oftentimes such entertainments
Were continued two or three days,
Till the dancers and their helpers
Were entirely exhausted.

Sev'ral years before my coming
Lands had been surveyed and platted.
Notice had been duly given
That in twenty-nine in autumn,
They would be put on the market.
When the Indians departed
For their winter hunting quarters,
They received the Agents warning
That in spring they must not come back.
All the settlers hoped they would not.
In this they were disappointed,

For they came again as usual,
Though not to the full in numbers.
Keokuk and those who followed
His advice were not among them.

Through that summer, eighteen-thirty,
I lived at the Indian village.
Sixteen Kickapoos, all young men,
Paid a visit to the Saukies,
And for thirty days were quartered
In one of the largest dwellings,
As the guests of all the village.
For some days before they left us
They made calls at all the wigwams.
When the time came for their going,
Each received a parting present
Of a horse to bear him homeward.

An event of note that season
Was a raid made by our Indians
On the Sioux at Turkey River,
Near where now Dubuque is standing.
Sev'ral Sioux braves fell before them,
And a Winnebago woman,—
A Menominee boy also.
Very strong were Winnebagoes,
And the Saukies hastened to them,
Cov'ring their mistake by giving
To them gifts of many horses.
The Menominees were friendly
And they spoke the Saukie language,
But as they lived at a distance
Settlement with them was put off
Till the coming of the spring-time.
Then nine leaders of the Foxes,
From an upper river village,
Went to make a fair adjustment.

The Menominees waylaid them
Made attack on them and killed them.
This stirred a revengeful spirit,
And in August our men fell on
The Menominees and slaughtered
Forty-six braves, squaws and children.[111]

Then the U. S. called our Indians
To account for this great slaughter,
As it surely had a right to
By the treaty terms, which stated
That all diff'rences arising
'Twixt these tribes should be submitted
To it, and by it be settled.

Keokuk, when called in council,
Took a stick and gave it balance
On his hand, and said in substance:
"Put these nine men, leading Foxes,
On one end, and on the other
Forty-six Menominees and
Then it will be fairly settled."

With the spring of thirty-one came
Indians in larger numbers,
And Black Hawk informed the settlers
That before another season
They must go below Rock River
Or above the pleasant valley.
All excepting Wells and Vandruff
Might remain throughout the season.

This move on the part of Black Hawk
Made it needful for the settlers
To consider what they might do
To insure their own protection.
Once before we had petitioned

Without notice being taken,
But we finally concluded
To put forth another effort.
So we drew up a petition,
Making therein formal statement
Of our grievances, including
Black Hawk's order for our going.
With the utmost haste we sent it
By a messenger to Belleville,
Where the Governor resided.

The effect which we desired
Was produced, and Governor Reynolds
Went to Federal Headquarters
At the Barracks near Saint Louis,
Where he notified the General
He could have the job of driving
Out the Indians, if he'd take it.
Otherwise the doughty Governor
Said that he himself would do it.

General Gaines took up the business,
And at once came to Rock Island
With a regiment of soldiers.
Though it had not been a practice
At the fort, the guns were fired
In the morning and the evening.
Also there was target shooting
In the day-time with the cannon.
All white families were brought in
With their horses and their cattle.

Then the General sent for Black Hawk,
With whom he had sev'ral parleys.
Black Hawk said he would not leave here,
And he would not fight to stay here,
But would sit down in his wigwam.
They could do with him as pleased them,

For himself he would do nothing;
From which General Gaines concluded
.That to fight was his intention.

All of General Gaines's forces,
With the soldiers on the island,
Only numbered some five hundred.
With another man I waited
On the General and suggested
That the settlers be enlisted,
And be called "Rock River Rangers."
This was done, and we were mustered
June, the fifth day, into service.
Benjamin J. Price was Captain;
J. W. Spencer, First Lieutenant;
Griffith Aubery, Second Lieutenant.
Leonard Bryant, Edwin Corbin
And James Haskins were the Sergeants.
Fifty-eight men were enlisted.

General Gaines now asked the Governor
For Militia reinforcements.
While awaiting their arrival,
He proceeded up Rock River
With the steamboat, Winnebago,
Having cannon mounted forward,
And a company of soldiers
On the deck, prepared for action.
Thus they passed the Indian village,
But no Indian man or woman,
And not even little children,
Gave to them the slightest notice.

When the troops of Governor Reynolds,
Numbering some sixteen hundred,
Reached a place ten miles below us
They encamped, and plans were laid there

For attack upon the Indians,
To be made upon the morrow.
It was thought they would be hiding
In the brush on Vandruff's Island.
General Gaines upon the steamboat,
With a company selected,
Was to come up the main channel;
Major Bliss was to bring over
From the fort the regular forces;
While the Governor's militia
Were to come upon the island
From the far side of the river.

We, who were Rock River Rangers,
Were with Major Bliss's forces,
And by him were formed and sent out
As the leaders of the column.
Marching near the present roadway
To the land of General Rodman,
We turned to the left, ascended
To the bluff, and thence proceeded
To the Watch Tower of the Black Hawk.
There we quickly planted cannon
And began to shell the island.

Very soon the General's steamboat
Reached the station as appointed
And joined in the cannonading,
But no Indians were discovered.
The militia, crossing over,
Found the village was deserted.
Having burned down all the wigwams,
They marched over near the fortress
And went into an encampment.

It was evident the Indians
Were beyond the Mississippi.
Soon Black Hawk was called in council

And a treaty was concluded
Whereby they agreed to stay there,
And the Government would give them
As much corn as could have been raised
By them had they stayed till harvest.
Rinnah Wells and I were chosen
To go over all their cornfields
And endeavor to determine
What amount they would have yielded.
It was sev'ral thousand bushels.

When we came to ask the Black Hawk
Why he did not keep his promise
To sit down within his wigwam
And allow them to do with him
As in any way might please them,
He replied that if the army
Under General Gaines had come there
He would certainly have done so;
But the Governor's militia
Had no discipline among them,
Therefore they could not be trusted.
In this thing he acted wisely,
For in the militia service
There were many frontier settlers,
Who had had friends killed by Indians
And were bitterly revengeful.

In the fol'wing spring, the Indians,
Nothwithstanding their agreement
To remain west side the river,
Crossed at Burlington and came up[112]
With all their canoes and horses,
As for years had been their custom.
Then the Government took notice.
General Atkinson was sent up
With a regiment of soldiers,
And arrived before the Indians.

They came on a few days after,
But kept south side of the river.
Wishing to observe their movements,
I crossed over there by fording.
Four young men I first encountered,
All with fine guns and equipment.
One was Se-us-kuk, the handsome
Son of the old Chieftain, Black Hawk.
Him I asked where they were going,
And he answered me by saying:
"Maybe to our own old village,
Or we may stop where we are now,
Or go farther up the river
To the village of the Prophet."

Then he asked if many soldiers
Were now at the fort. I told him
That there were a goodly number.
Finally they made encampment
Two miles farther up the river.

Next day at the fort we heard them,
Beating on their drums and singing,
Though their camp was five miles from us
And the hills were intervening.

General Atkinson was anxious
To inform the frontier settlers
Of their danger, and I offered
To go out with his dispatches.
Wishing to avoid the Indians,
I dropped down the Mississippi
In a light canoe, and landed
Just below Rock River's entrance.
Having carefully secreted
My canoe among the willows,
For the settlements I started.

All alone I camped the first night.
Forty miles on foot the next day
Brought me to the nearest settlers,
And from them I went to others.
This my message was in substance:
That there doubtless would be conflict
With the Indians, and the settlers
All should seek a place of safety.
Coming back I had good fortune,
My canoe was where I'd hid it,
And I soon was on the island.

We had thought that here the General
With his force would stop the Indians.
This he did not do, but called on
Governor Reynolds for assistance.
He soon came with eighteen hundred
Mounted men.   Three hundred others
Were in rendezvous at Dixon.

Everything was now depending
On the movements of the General.
Two large keel boats were secured,
Also several Mackinaw boats.
These were loaded with provisions,
And on May the eighth we started
On the warlike expedition.

.   .   .   .   .   .

Statements have been made about us,
Which have had wide circulation,
In regard to our abusing
Indians, both men and women.
These are basely false, if not so
Never have I known about them.

Our relation to the Indians,
After the first summer season,
Might be counted as peculiar.
Having to our lands good title
From the Government, we felt that
We of right should be protected.
On the other hand, the Indians
Claimed the land with much assurance.
Living thus almost three seasons,
Without any serious outbreak,
Seems to me a flat'ring record
Both for white men and for Indians.

XV. THE BLACK HAWK WAR,—
PRELIMINARIES

PLANNING TO RETAKE SAUKENAUK[113]

WHEN The Hawk made his physical exit, he still
    Was obsessed in his mind: he had purpose and will
In some way or other his town to regain,
And all of his rights as an Indian maintain.

It was lightly indeed that he settled down
On the Iowa River near Keokuk's town;
And at once with all of his skill he began
To form his connections and perfect his plan.

Through the Chief and Head Man with Davenport's aid,
Application to visit the Father was made,
That the Black Hawk himself the story might tell
And plead for the village that he loved so well.

No answer came back, and the old Chieftain then
Turned his thoughts to a warlike solution again.
From a visit to Malden Nahpope had returned:[114]
His report was so good, that the warrior's heart burned
With desire a great combination to form,
That should sweep back the whites with the force of a storm.

Already had agents and runners been sent
To the Indian tribes the great cause to present.
They had been well received, and an answer came back,
That help would appear when he made an attack.

After seeing the Prophet, a visit was paid
To Malden, in hopes that the British might aid
In his plan; but they said that they now were at peace,

And advised that he also from warfare should cease,
And in full hope of justice his cause should present
To his Washington Father, the great President.

The Black Hawk was persistent. He went here and there
Arousing an int'rest, in hopes that a share
Would be taken at length in the on-coming strife,
By those in whose cause he had once risked his life.

Before Black Hawk returned, Nahpope went again.
His counsel was largely with second class men:
What they thought should be done, he considered they said
Would be done, and out of his own fertile head
He made up details that would bring to his Chief
The greatest delight and the greatest relief.

Not long after Black Hawk, half doubtful, came back,
Nahpope, with good medicine, followed his track.
He stopped with the Prophet to fix his report,
Then sought the new village, avoiding the fort.

Nahpope's Report to Black Hawk

From our great Prophet, Winneshiek,
    Good news to you I bring:
The British Father by express
    Has said that in the spring

He'll prove to you beyond a doubt
    He is your constant friend,
And all the things that you will need
    To you by boats he'll send.

Milwaukee will be landing place
    And there a store you'll find:
Arms, ammunition, clothing, food,—
    Supplies of every kind.

The Prophet says he has received
  The wampum belts from these:
The Ottawas and Chippewas
  And Pottawatomies.

The Winnebagoes strength is known,
  And well known through the land:
Each one of these without reserve,
  He has at his command.

In case of possible defeat,
  Chief Was-sa-cu-mi-co,
Of Canada, will welcome us,—
  To Selkirk we may go.

But we can suffer no defeat,—
  We're sure of victory:
The issue we must bravely meet,
  And we shall happy be.

.　.　.　.　.　.

Long after Nahpope sweetly slept,
The old Black Hawk his vigil kept,
And yet he was a happy man:
All things were favoring his plan;
The Prophet was his truest friend,
And he would trust him to the end.

.　.　.　.　.　.

With the wonderful news that Nahpope had brought
Black Hawk to stir up the Saukie tribe sought.
But their Chief and Head Man did not seem much inclined
To regard it, and bluntly he spoke out his mind:
"They are liars, these men: they impose upon you,
And with them you ought to have nothing to do."

But Black Hawk preferred the advice and the news,
That most fully met his desires and views;
And whatever Keokuk might have to say,
He resolved to proceed on his own chosen way.

The Pottawatomie and Winnebago Council at Indiantown on the Site of Tiskilwa

On the tenth of February,
    Eighteen hundred thirty-two,
Indians gathered in a council
    To decide what they should do,

As to joining in a movement
    To drive back the white man's tide,
That upon their lands the red men
    Might continue to abide.

There were present Winnebagoes,
    Pottawatomies as well:
Black Hawk, from the Sacs and Foxes,
    Came about his plans to tell.

With him were his chief Lieutenant,
    Nahpope, bitter partizan,
And the Winnebago Prophet,
    Chief abettors of the plan.

Winneshiek, the Indian Prophet,
    In the council took the lead:
He was eloquent and earnest,
    And to him they all gave heed.

"Join this movement with our brother,"
    Loud the gifted Prophet cried,
"Only thus can we continue,—
    We should rally to his side.

"If our tribes are all united
    We shall be like forest trees,
And our loud, victorious war cry
    Shall be borne on every breeze."

Shabbona responded briefly:[115]
    "With Black Hawk my spirit grieves;
But too well we know the white men
    Number forces as the leaves.

"We can not contend against them.
    Let all thoughts of warfare cease:
Though we know not what may wait us,
    Better is the path of peace."

Shabbona was Chief and Head Man
    Of the Pottawatomies;
But Waubonsie was the War Chief
    And Black Hawk he wished to please.

All the other Chiefs assembled
    Stood with Shabbona, Head Man,
And by vote it was decided
    Not to fall in with the plan.

ACTIONS AND REACTIONS

When the council had ended, with sorrowful heart,
Black Hawk to his wigwam was quick to depart;
But the Prophet and Nahpope with courage went forth
To continue their work farther on to the north.
Some Chiefs took their wampum and answered, in short,
That if war should break out they would give their support.

Returning to Black Hawk they brought the good news,
That he had but to start, and all tribes would enthuse:
It was action they wanted, let him but proceed
And all the red forces would rally with speed.

The old Chief, with the help of the shrewd Winneshiek,
Was able more fully his plans to complete,
Including, as seems from a later report,
A project by which he might capture the fort.

Black Hawk at the fortress made several calls,
But was never permitted inside of its walls:
The Prophet was also a caller,—no doubt
The things that he wanted to know he found out.

There were various spies in the Indian bands,
And some of them played into white men's hands:
Black Hawk's preparations were quite as well known
In Keokuk's town as they were in his own,
And men in the fortress were not left in doubt
As to what the persistent old man was about.

Major Bliss, Commandant, and the wise Davenport
Called the settlers about to come into the fort,
Or the trading house, round which the Colonel had made
Of logs set on end a secure stockade.

The Battle of the Giants

Meanwhile the Black Hawk had made ready to move
With all of his people, and bravely to prove
What he long had contended was Indian right
By a full exhibition of Indian might.

The first thing to do was the nearest at hand,
To gather recruits out of Keokuk's band:
It would be a hard task, but his reason therefor
Was great, and he knew that the Saukies loved war,—
He would plead with them all before Keokuk's face,
And woe be to him who was false to his race.

With the highest of hopes they started away
To begin their great work on that fair April day.

BLACK HAWK

KEOKUK

WAPELLO

SHABBONA

h

The braves in their feathers and paint were arrayed,
And their weapons of war were all fully displayed;
Black Hawk in the lead wore a soldier's red coat,
And the flag of Great Britain was proudly afloat.
They carried a war-post with them as they went,
And planted it near to Chief Keokuk's tent.

All the Indians assembled, a literal host,
And stood in a circle around the war-post.
With a loud whoop the Black Hawk, as few others could,
Hurled his hatchet,—it sank to the head in the wood.
Lesser Chiefs sent their weapons like rain through the air
To find place by the side of their great leader's there,
While shouts of defiance and hate rose on high,
Sufficient to rend the great vault of the sky.

The Chieftains drew back. Then with leap and with bound
And the wildest of war whoops the braves circled round,
In turn darting forward to strike the war-stake,
And thus individual enlistments to make.

In the midst of the tumult the Black Hawk appeared
By the side of the post, and the multitude cheered.
His hour had come, and in eloquent stream
His spirit poured forth on his favorite theme.

He told of the days when the Saukies had roved
As they would o'er the land, warred, hunted and loved,
With joy in their hearts, and secure in the rights
Which the Great Spirit gave. Then he spoke of the whites,
Who had come from afar and has posed as their friends,
But had only done so to accomplish their ends.

They had put forth their laws, and had wheedled the Sauks
Into signing their treaties whene'er they had talks.
They had claimed that these said what they wished them
        to say,
And with soldiers had driven the Saukies away;
They had brought to the village the white men instead,

And were running their plows through the graves of their
          dead;
They had beaten the women and even the men,
And misused and abused them again again and again;
Even he had been charged with shooting a hog,
And beaten with sticks like a trembling dog.

Then he cried, "Why is this? It is simply because
We're divided and held by the white's evil laws.
But it need not be so. If we only unite
We can throw off the yoke, and establish our right.
Let us show we are Sauks, that we truly are men,
And we can possess our old village again.
We have but to strike and the tribes will arise,
The British will aid, we will capture the prize,
A great League of Nations will hold back the whites,
And forever preserve all the Indian rights."
When he ceased there was stillness, a moment of pause,
Then the very ground shook with the roar of applause.
The crowd was inflamed, the excitement ran high
And, "Nahpope! Let Nahpope be heard," was the cry.

The Prophet's half brother was quick to respond,
For of public address he had always been fond.
He leaped to the front, and with thunderous tone,
In the name of the Prophet as well as his own,
He told in the most circumstantial detail
Of the goods that the British would bring without fail,
Of tobacco and wampum that all tribes had sent,[116]
And of greatest success in the final event.

With clamorous cries the war-crazy host
Surged around the tomahawk-bristled war-post,
And those who had made up the Saukie peace band,
United in loud and insistent demand
That their great Chief should lead them away to the fight,
Which was soon to be on between red men and white.

When Keokuk heard, without any delay
He strode from his place,—all before him gave way.
Advancing he laid his left hand on the post,
And the heavens were rent with the cries of the host.

He raised his right hand.   All was still, and he said
In his rich, measured tones: "You wish to be led
'Gainst the whites, who are plowing the graves of our dead,
Who through the long years have outraged and wronged
Our people, and seized what to us has belonged.
I sympathize with you, and wish that our might
Were sufficient to change every wrong into right;
But the white men are strong, and their numbers are great,
And to move against them is to seal our own fate.

"Every warrior and brave, who a hatchet can throw,
Or carry a gun on the war path must go,
And going expect never more to return
While waters shall flow or fires shall burn.

"As your Chief and Head Man, 'tis incumbent on me
When you make choice of peace, your Father to be;
But when you choose war, 'tis my duty to lead
You forth to the conflict, and be first in deed.

"If war is your choice, I am willing to go,
On this sole condition, which each one must know:
That first, with our hatchets, our spears and our knives,
We kill our infirm and our children and wives,
And in graves by the village we tenderly lay
Their poor, mangled bodies in silence away,—
By the love that we bear them such sacrifice make,
And then go to war, dire vengeance to take
On the dastardly whites, and water the ground
With our blood, till on earth not a Saukie is found."

Then he turned to the Black Hawk: "Venerable sir,
Have I not spoken well, and do not you concur?
You have been a great War Chief for years, and you know

That war means to take as to give the death blow.
Whatever the force we are able to send
The whites will send greater, and win in the end.
Your heart is so hot for the cause that you love,
That you do not give heed to the Spirit above;
But the falsehoods that come from those who would deceive,
And compass your ruin you're fain to believe.

"You must know, O great leader of men, that the peace
'Twixt the British and Long Knives for years shall not cease;
And the red men you think will join you in your raid
Will preserve their own peace, and not come to your aid.

"By the great name you bear, I beseech you to-day
To turn from your evil advisers away,
To forsake the war path, all your plottings to cease,
And to follow the broad way of honor and peace.
The spring time has come, and the ground cries for seed.
Go back to your village, be Father indeed
To your people, look after the good of your band,
And be happy with them in this Iowa land."

The great orator ceased, and a silence profound,
Like a benison fell on the Saukies around,
Affection and reason and judgment had sway,
And no one thought it needful aught further to say.

The old Chief was dejected, his prospects were black.
How could he go forward?   He would not turn back.
Not a warrior from Keokuk's band had he gained,
While some of his own in the village remained.
In darkness had set the bright sun of the morn,—
He had come forth to shear, but he went away shorn.[117]

CROSSING THE RUBICON

Black Hawk gathered his people
    Between the water and wood,
By the side of the old ruined chimney,
    Where once Fort Madison stood

He rounded them up with his warriors,
    And sentinels posted each day
To guard against any defections,
    Before they should move on their way.

They crossed the great Mississippi,
    At a place that was called Yellow Banks;
Then slowly they made their way northward,
    In broken, irregular ranks.[118]

Some distance below the Rock River
    They were met by the shrewd Winneshiek;
And when they went into encampment,
    He stood up before them to speak:

"O warriors and braves of the great Saukie tribe,
Whose devotion and courage no tongue can describe,
Your fortunes look up, you shall find better fate:
Follow us as true braves, and your gain shall be great.
The White Beaver may come, but he'll not interfere
With our movements as long as we peaceful appear.
We are not ready yet to act otherwise:
We must go up Rock River to spring our surprise.
Reinforcements will come to our brave little band,
And the White Beaver's army we then can withstand."

On the morning of April eleventh
    They went up Rock River's south side,
And encamped south east of the village,
    Where again they hoped to abide.

Black Hawk and his well mounted warriors
    To the great river wended their way;
And there in full view of the fortress,
    They remained till the close of the day.

Then slowly they passed to the eastward,
    By the ford to the island they crossed,

And soon in the dark of the forest
　　To the eyes of the spies they were lost.[119]

Their ways through the pathways familiar,
　　With the greatest of caution they made
To a grove that was east of the fortress,
　　And south of the trader's stockade.

It has been supposed they intended
　　To wait till the coming of light,
Blow up the east gate from the cavern[120]
　　Rush in through the breaches, and fight

With all of their wild, savage power
　　In a thunderbolt, capture the fort,
And rouse all the Indian nations
　　To war by their runners' report.

EXCITEMENT AT THE TRADING HOUSE

When the spies brought the news of their crossing
　　To the newly constructed stockade,
All present were fully persuaded
　　That the Saukies intended a raid.

On the trading house.　Though well protected
　　By the logs, they began to enquire
What to do if the Indian arrows
　　On the roof should enkindle a fire.

The well was without, and in order
　　That a water supply should not fail,
All hands set to work till each barrel
　　Was filled, and each kettle and pail.

Josepha, the medicine woman,
　　Squaw wife of the Frenchman, Gouquy,
As a spy went forth in the darkness,
　　Her skill for the whites to employ.

The notes of the whippoorwills calling,
    Soon fell on her delicate ear:
Too early it was for their coming,
    And she knew that the Indians were near.

She did not return until midnight;
    But then she was ready to say,
That she thought all danger was over
    Till the time for the dawning of day.

ATKINSON AND KEOKUK TO THE RESCUE

In the meantime Keokuk, fearing
    That issues of death might betide,
With a force of his own chosen warriors,
    Went up on the Iowa side.

The night of April eleventh
    Came dark, with abundance of rain,
And twenty miles down by the river
    His force was compelled to remain.

. . . . . .

Others slept; but Keokuk watching,
    About the noon of the night,
Far down on the great river's bosom,
    Saw the bleam of an on-coming light.

It glowed from the prows of the steamboats,
    That the troops of the White Beaver bore:
The Chief wakened Smart and with torches,
    They signaled the boats to the shore.

Explanations were made, and The Beaver
    Gave orders for planks to be lowered:
They were quickly obeyed, and the Saukies
    Were hastily taken aboard.

It was two o'clock in the morning,
  (Long before the return of the sun,)
When the boats came up to the island,
  And fired the glad signal-gun.

A salute was returned from the fortress,
  That was followed by heartiest cheers:
Reinforcements had come, and rejoicing
  At once took the place of all fears.

. . . . . .

At the trading house thunder and cannon
  Were mingled, but shouting was clear:
They thought that the fortress had fallen,
  And the bravest were smitten with fear.

Elder Kinney, who came from Port Byron,
  Suggested that all join in prayer;
But the Frenchman responded, indignant,
  "Much more do we need ze wattair."

Black Hawk and His Band Go Up Rock River

Whatever the plan of the Black Hawk
  That might have matured with the light,
He cared not to contend with large forces,
  But departed while yet it was night.[121]

The squaws were meanwhile on the hillside,
  For affection their footsteps had led
To their own dearly loved Chip-pi-an-nock,
  Where lay the remains of their dead.

With the first gray dawn of the morning
  To the camp returned women and men,
And gathering up their belongings,
  They journeyed up river again.

Before they went into encampment,
  A messenger came from the band,
With orders direct from The Beaver,
  To go back to the Iowa land.

Black Hawk returned word that he would not;
  But early the following morn,
Would peaceably go up the river,
  At the Prophet's request to make corn.

They went on, but another expressman
  Brought word they must halt in their course
And go back in peace, or The Beaver
  Would come and eject them by force.

This roused the old Chief and his people,
  Who felt that their conduct was right;
And they sent back word to The Beaver
  To come on if he wished for a fight.

Arriving at Winneshiek's village,
  By the Indians there they were pressed,
Whate'er they might do in the future,
  To remain a short time for a rest.

This they did, but Sub-Agent Gratiot,
  Third messenger who had been sent,
Told them kindly and plainly, The Beaver
  Their failure to heed would resent:

He would come if need be with an army,
  And compel them the river to cross.
As their friend the sub-agent urged them
  To go while they could without loss.

By this time their anger was kindled,
  A feeling of hatred was rife;
And only by aid of the Prophet
  Did Gratiot escape with his life.

The chief Winnebagoes told Black Hawk,
   If the white men did not interfere,
He might stay, if he wished, with the Prophet
   And make his corn crop for the year.

They were not disposed to assist him
   In the cause for which he had come forth;
But plainly told him they desired
   That he would not go farther north.

The old Chief was much disconcerted,
   And hardly knew what he would do:
Pottawatomies should be consulted,
   They might help him to see the thing through.

The next day they left for Kishwaukee,
   And when they encamped for the night,
He called all his chief men about him
   And revealed their desperate plight.

He said they had met with deception,
   And waked to a fearful surprise,
That all the fair pledges through Nahpope
   Had proved to be nothing but lies.

But the truth must be held as a secret
   From the people till some future day:
Pottawatomies must be consulted,
   And given a chance for their say.

The next morning they told all the people
   That news from Milwaukee had come,
And a Chief from the great British Father
   Would assist in regaining their home.

Atkinson's Arrangements

The General's ostensible purpose
  Was to apprehend if he could
The murderers, Saukies and Foxes,
  Who had shed the Menominees blood.[122]

He called upon Wapello, Fox Chief
  And Keokuk, Saukie Chief, then,
To find and bring in and surrender
  The leaders of these bloody men.

He sent to Governor Reynolds
  A request, by a messenger's hand,
For state militia assistance
  In expelling Black Hawk and his band.

Going up by boat to Fort Crawford,
  He secured reinforcements from thence,[123]
And by messenger warned all the settlers
  To prepare as they could for defence.

Returning he met with the friendlys,
  And Wapello gave up three men,
Who in the Menominees' slaughter,
  Accounted as leaders had been.

This matter now seemed less important,
  So the friendly Indians were told
That the men would have generous treatment,
  Which they did, for they soon were paroled.

The Enlistment of State Troops

On the sixteenth of April the Governor sent out
A call for militia to rally about
The standard, at Beardstown upon the sixth day

From the time of the call, for the driving away
Of Black Hawk and his troublesome pro-British band,
Who with warlike intent had invaded the land.
He also called out a large force to appear
At Dixon's that they might protect the frontier.

The answer was prompt.   Nearly two thousand men
Dropped their work and appeared at the rendezvous; when
They had been organized they started away:
It was April the seven and twentieth day.[124]

O'er the prairie they went, through the waters they passed
Till they reached Yellow Banks on the river at last.
There they waited three days for provisions, and when
These had come, they pushed on toward the fortress again.

At the mouth of Rock River they went into camp,
June seventh as dews of the evening fell damp.
General Atkinson met them, and there the brigade
Took the oath, and Federal soldiers were made.

On the ninth they were ordered to Dixon's to find
The Indians, and fight, should Black Hawk be inclined:
The regular troops were by boats to ascend,
In hopes to arrive ere the conflict should end.

Their orders received, on the very same day
In a frolicsome mood they started away.
On the next afternoon they reached Prophets town:
No Indians were there, and they burned the huts down.
Pushing on a few miles they encamped for the night,
Still anxious to find the bold Saukies and fight.

Some spies they had sent, through an Indian had heard
That Black Hawk was near Dixon's,—they brought back
          the word.
The troopers knew well for what purpose they came,

And with valorous zeal their hearts were aflame.
One purpose they had, the Black Hawk to o'ertake
And their baggage they left that more speed they might
    make.

A POTTAWATOMIE COUNCIL

About May First

When at his own village Chief Shabbona learned
That Black Hawk and his people had really returned,
He was fearful of warfare, and with no surcease
He put forth every effort that might make for peace.
Here and there on his pony in great haste he sped,
Consulting with white men as well as with red.
A council was held, and a statement was made
That all Pottawatomies, who should give aid
To Black Hawk and his band in the course of the war,
By the tribe should be counted as traitors therefor.

BLACK HAWK'S MEETING WITH SHABBONA
AND WAUBONSIE

May 13th

As soon as Black Hawk reached the Kishwaukee Creek
A runner was sent his old comrades to seek,
Waubonsie and Shabbona, who once had brought
Their service to Britain, and gallantly fought.

They answered the summons and came to the band,
Where every one sought to take them by the hand,
And heap on them terms of endearment and pride,
As brothers and friends who would be on their side.

At the wigwam of Black Hawk a dinner was spread,
While the flag of Great Britain was floating o'erhead.
As they ate, by the squaws entertainment was made
With songs, drums and rattles, a rude serenade.

The meal being over the Chieftains withdrew
To a place in the woodland, to talk matters through.
They seated themselves and Black Hawk told again
Of the wrongs he had suffered from grasping white men,
And appealed to the Chieftains to rally their bands
And give aid in a war to recover his lands:

"At Saukenauk my life began,
And there I lived as youth and man.
I loved the place its tower high,
Its mighty rivers flowing by,
Its shady groves and prairies green,
The whole a most delightful scene.
There was my father's body laid,
And there my children's graves were made:
There I desired to live and die,
And there I hoped my bones would lie.

"But to my village white men came;
They seized upon it without shame,
And in my old age drove me forth,
As though my claims were of no worth.
Mine is to-day and exile's lot:
I can not look on that loved spot.

"Think not that you in peace can stay.
Ere many moons shall pass away,
The shameless white men will demand
That you give up to them your land.
Your happy days will then be done,
Your path lie toward the setting sun:
Hence you must go with all your braves,
While white men plow your fathers' graves.

"Now is the time for you to act,
Before such things shall be in fact.
Join force with me, help me regain
My village: it is very plain,

That when the white men see our strength
They will not fight, but will at length
Treat with us: thus my home I'll gain
And you your fair lands will retain.

"As brothers we have always been,—
United we can surely win.
Beside the British we have fought
Against those who our lands have sought,
Beneath the same robe we have slept,
The same religious feasts have kept,
Have gone together after game,—
To-day our interests are the same.

"My runners have gone far and near,
And called the Chiefs to gather here.
To-morrow I'll a dog-feast make,
And ask them all our part to take.
If you in this affair will lead,
We'll have a force the whites must heed:
Their warlike efforts they will cease,
And soon make overtures for peace."

Pathetic and earnest was Black Hawk that day;
'Twas the very last card that was left him to play:
Pottawatomie help he must have at all cost,
And failing to gain it his cause would be lost.
When he ceased many moments of silence went by,
Then slowly old Shabbona made his reply:

"Our friend and our brother, your speech we have heard,
We have listened with care and have weighed every word.
You have made to us here a most eloquent plea,
And with much you have said we can fully agree;
But the day has long passed when the red man can stand
'Gainst the on-coming whites in defense of their land.
It matters not how, when or where we unite,
How crafty we are or how well we may fight;

The white men as a class are as valiant as we,
And in numbers as great as the waves of the sea;
Their weapons of war are much better than ours;
Their supplies are much greater, and all of their powers:
They may lose at the first, but they still will contend
And you may be sure they will win in the end.

"My great-uncle, Pontiac, gallantly fought
To withstand them, but all that he did came to naught.
Tecumseh, it seemed for a time, plotted well;
But he failed, and I stood by his side when he fell.
In defeat, the command of his braves came to me;
There was naught I could do but give orders to flee.
Before the Great Spirit I then made a vow
Not to fight with the whites.   I have kept it till now.

"I sympathize with you, my brother and friend,
Though I know all too well it is vain to contend,
And that if I join you, as you think I should,
It will ruin my people and do you no good.
I can not be here when you hold your dog-feast,
Or help to advance your war plans in the least.
For yourself and your people it surely is best
The White Beaver to heed, and return to the west."

Waubonsie sat solemnly smoking, the while
The others were speaking, in Indian style;
Then he quietly spoke to the Black Hawk, "You know
At the council last winter I voted to go
With you on the war path to help in your need:
All the others said, 'no,' and their voice I must heed.
With Shabbona, now, I am bound to agree.
No hope of success in your plan I can see;
But to-morrow I'll come to the council you hold,
As befits a War Chief, who is faithful and bold."

JOHN REYNOLDS
Governor of Illinois

HENRY DODGE
Governor of Wisconsin

WILLIAM CLARKE
Governor of Missouri Territory

JOHN CHAMBERS
Governor of Iowa Territory

k

XVI. THE BLACK HAWK WAR,
EARLIER STAGES

May 12th

WHEN the Governor reached Dixon's Ferry he found
Majors Stillman and Bailey encamped on the ground.
To the call he had sent they had given good heed
And had mustered their troops with commendable speed.

Colonel Dodge had arrived with his Michigan band[126]
To consult, and as needed to lend a brave hand.
Other prominent men had come in to observe
And to learn how they might most efficiently serve.

These men were consulted. They said that a scout
Had reported the Indians were scattered about,
In an effort to gain both recruits and supplies.
To move on them now did not seem to be wise.

STILLMAN'S DEFEAT

May 14th

The forces of Stillman and Bailey were keen
To move before Atkinson came on the scene
Not having been sworn as U. S. volunteers,
They were still state militia, as clearly appears;
And they pleaded with Reynolds to give them a chance
To go forth, and his fame with their own to enhance.
"The Old Ranger" consented, whate'er his belief,
And an order made out as Commander in Chief.[127]

With great hope they started the following day,
Well armed and equipped for a deadly affray.

173

13

On the next day out in the afternoon
They camped on the branch of a creek, and soon,
Without any thought of a soldier's care,
They began their evening meal to prepare.

Meanwhile the Black Hawk, up the river at least
Four miles, was serving his friends a dog-feast;
But his hope to rally his race had fled:
He was ready to parley for peace instead.

A runner who had just returned came to say
A large body of horsemen were eight miles away.
As soon as he heard the report of the scout,
Three braves with a white flag the Black Hawk sent out,
In his name the on-coming soldiers to greet,
And ask them with himself and his warriors to meet
At his camp or their own in a council of peace,
That all thought of further contention might cease.
He also sent five of his young men to see
What reception was given the flag-bearing three.

When the braves, who were charged with the message,
     appeared
At the camp they were seized, for the soldiers feared
This, that or the other, they knew not what,
"Some kind of a devilish Indian plot."

They told their story as well as they could,
But it seems it was not very well understood,
And the upshot was that they were detained
Until the whole matter could be explained.

On the hillside away about a half mile
Some horsemen were seen in Indian file:
They were the five watchers the Black Hawk had sent,
And against them a mob of the raw rangers went,
An irregular, headstrong, reckless band,

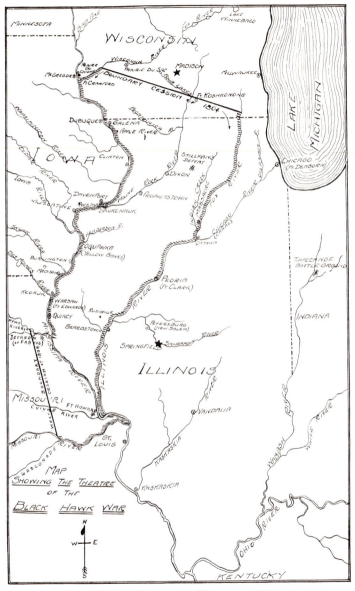

MAP OF THE CESSION UNDER THE TREATY OF 1804 AND THE
THEATRE OF THE BLACK HAWK WAR

Drawn by Ben H. Wilson

Without restraint and without command.
They had come with a horde of red men to fight,
And now was their chance, for lo, five were in sight.

The red horsemen patiently waited until
They felt sure the white men were coming to kill,
Then they turned from the scene to seek safety in flight,
And whipped up their ponies with all of their might;
But ere they had gone very far o'er the plain
The hindermost two were o'ertaken and slain.

The others reached camp, and the Black Hawk received
Their report, and although it could scarce be believed,
The on-coming soldiers themselves were the proof.
Only one thing remained for the Indians' behoof,
And the old Chieftain stationed his little command
In ambush, the charge of the whites to withstand.

When the rangers swept up, the Indians fired
Their guns, and let out their war whoop as required.
To the shot and the yell the pursuers gave heed;
They reversed their direction and doubled their speed;
The pursuers at once the Indians became,
And they acted the part to their undying fame.

At the camp of the whites great confusion prevailed:
Their ears by the cries of their friends were assailed,
And the blood-curdling whoops of Black Hawk's little band
Made them think the whole tribe of the Sauks was at hand.
In an instant the camp like a bedlam became;
Some shot at the envoys, a black deed of shame;
A ball took effect, and one Saukie fell dead,
The others escaped in the tumult and fled.

In panic the soldiers lost heart and lost mind,
They leaped on their horses and rode like the wind:
By one thought of escape they all were possessed,
And each made an effort to outstrip the rest.

The night had come on, but the light of the moon,
Which gave its pale beams, was to them a real boon,
And before the sunrise set the east in a flame,
Alone and in groups to the ferry they came,
Except about forty, who took other ways
And could not be heard from for several days.

No tales were alike when the stragglers arrived
At the ferry that night, as those who had survived
A terrible fight with a force of red men
Far greater than theirs, from two times to ten.

But heroes there were on that day of disgrace,
And they were of those who deserve a high place
In the list of the brave, when the names are set down
Of those who have won the great meed of renown.

Captain Adams stood forth with a handful of men
In the path of the foe, where a troop should have been:
With no thought of flight, they fought on that ground
And there the next day their dead bodies were found.[128]

Governor Reynolds Takes Action

With the promptness and vigor by which he was known,
For his error the Governor sought to atone.
All hope of immediate coercion was past;
For weeks or for months the contention must last;
Majors Stillman and Bailey could do nothing more,
And little indeed their discredited corps;
In the rest of the force disaffection was rife,—
They had more heart for home than for Indian strife.[129]

"The Old Ranger" considered these matters, and then
He wrote out a call for two thousand new men
To gather for service in twenty-five days;
He charged Colonel Strode of Galena to raise
Such a force as was needed to guard the frontier

Against any attack he had reason to fear;
He wrote Colonel Dodge, who was camping near by,
Of Stillman's disaster, that he might supply
Such protection for Michigan people as he
Might think, 'gainst the danger, sufficient to be.

To the General, ascending the river by boat,
An account of the Stillman disaster he wrote,
And he earnestly urged that the General would
Note their needs, and push onward as fast as he could.

Major Horn he sent down to Saint Louis to see
Colonel March and arrange for provisions to be
Sent up to Fort Wilburn with care and with speed,
That they might be on hand for the new army's need;
Major Adams he ordered at once to obtain
For the horses sufficient supplies of good grain.

All this work was accomplished while yet it was night,
And his messengers left with the coming of light.

For breakfast that morning provisions were scant:
Dixon slaughtered his cattle to meet the great want,
For the army that day to the far field must go
To bury the dead and to seek for the foe.

They arrived at the place a short time before night,
And there they beheld a most terrible sight:
The dead bodies of those whom the Saukies had slain
Were horribly mangled and strewn o'er the plain.

They gathered them up with the tenderest care
And, nine men in one grave, they buried them there:
Two others, who singly had fallen that day,
They interred where they fell, some distance away.

The army that night encamped on the ground,
While Henry's spy troop searched the country around;

The Indians however had gone far away,
And the army returned to its base the next day.

The General had not arrived with supplies,
The soldiers were restless and not always wise,
And such of them as did not wish to remain
In the service were somewhat inclined to complain.

The next morning the Governor strongly appealed
To the murmuring men to remain in the field,
To guard against ravages on the frontier
Until the new levy of troops should appear.

The forces of Stillman consented to stay,
And were made the Fifth Regiment that very day:
They chose Captain Johnson as Colonel to serve,
And they strictly agreed his commands to observe.

The same afternoon the General appeared
With stores in abundance, and every one cheered:
Good feeling prevailed, all murmuring ceased,
And no soldier requested that he be released.

Black Hawk Spares Elijah Kilbourne the Second Time

Two scouts were taken prisoners
  From Stillman's beaten force.
One sought to flee, but was shot down:
  The other's fate was worse,

Or so he apprehended that
  It certainly would be,
For he was bound with strongest cords
  And fastened to a tree.

The Indians moved by savage hate
  Were glad to "treat him rough:"
Full many an insult he received,
  And many a kick and cuff.

The great Chief passing looked on him,
  (Their eyes a moment met,)
He spoke in low tones, "Do not think
  That Black Hawk will forget."

He came again, unloosed the cords,
  And acting as a guide,
In silence strode on till they came
  To Rocky River's side.

Then Black Hawk spoke, "Though I should kill,
  I yet will let you live:
You proved unfaithful as a son,
  But Black Hawk can forgive.

"Go tell your Chieftain that I came,
  Not to provoke a fight;
But simply to assert a claim
  To what was mine by right.

"His soldiers basely fired upon
  My white flag yesterday,
And slew its bearers. I will fight
  Till I am called away."

Black Hawk Sends Out His Warriors

May 15th

At Stillman's Run the die had been cast;
The issue was joined, it was well known at last.
Brave blood had been spilled, both of red men and white;
They must fight to the end, be that end what it might.

The old Chieftain small bodies of warriors sent out
To prey on the settlers scattered about.
Before in their sev'ral directions they sped,
He called them around him and solemnly said:

"This is the time to win renown
And gain the great bag handed down.
Go, show yourselves true braves to be;
Go, and avenge our murdered three."

He also sent runners to follow the track
Of old Shabbona, note what he did and come back;
And orators, smooth-tongued, to seek every band
Of bold Pottawatomies throughout the land,
And urge them to rise and to sing their war songs,
And improve the occasion to right all their wrongs.

SHABBONA'S RIDE

May 15th

At the midnight hour great Shabbona lay
When a messenger came to report the affray
At Stillman's Run, with the utter rout
Of the whites by the reds, and the sending out
Of runners by Black Hawk to bands round about,

Appealing to them to arise up and fight
In the Indian way for their race and their right.
Great Shabbona knew what the slaughter would be,
If unwarned were the settlers, and hastily he
Roused his nephew, young Pyps, and his son, Pypegee.

To the Fox River region bold Pypegee went,
While to Holderman's Grove the brave Pyps was sent.
How little they knew that their young lives would pay
To the Sauks' bloody band in a land far away
For the fair deed of mercy they did on that day!

The great Chief chose himself the cabins to seek
Near the banks of "The Bureau" and Indian Creek.
The night dews were damp as he started away,
And he made many miles ere the dawning of day,
For the need it was great, and would brook no delay.

The white foam stood out on his panting steed,
That was doing its best to meet the great need:
Thus Shabbona rode with the speed of the wind,
Bareheaded, his long hair streaming behind,
With the fate of the settlers always in mind.

The broad prairie was like a rich carpet of green,
Here and there the bright flowers in beauty were seen;
But he gave not a thought to the flowers or grass,
To the deep, swollen stream or the miry morass:
On, over or through 'twas his purpose to pass.

Not far from where now is the town of La Moille
Squire Dimmick was turning the rich prairie soil,
When the Indian horseman burst on his sight,
Rode up to his side and proceeded to 'light,
And pour into his ears the tale of affright.

But the white man was not to be easily stirred:
He listened at length to the Chief's broken word,
And then said: "I can see no great cause for alarm.
Last year I was warned, but there followed no harm.
There is work to be done, I must stay on the farm,

"At least until I shall have planted my corn.
I thank you, my friend, for your effort to warn."
But Shabbona said: "If yourself you will stay,
Send quickly your squaw and pappooses away
Or they will be dead ere there comes a new day."

Thus speaking, he sprang to the saddle, and then
He turned for a moment to Dimmick again
And, lifting his hand, cried out: "So-ho!
Auhaw puckegee, you must go,
Or fall before dawn 'neath the Indians' blow."

Then away at a gallop the messenger passed,
But the message had stirred the young farmer at last:

Though a lion in courage, unwilling to cower,
In his wagon he started within the next hour
And soon was beyond the dread savages' power.

The next place to which the great Shabbona went
Was the neat cabin home of John L. Ament,
Who responded at once to the note of alarm:
With his wife at his side and his babe on his arm,
Well mounted, he fled from all danger of harm.

From thence the great Chief in his merciful race
Dashed on at high speed to the Chamberlain place
And, having warned him, he proceeded forthwith
To the homes of Eli and Elijah Smith,
Of Epperson, Doolittle, Mosely and Myth.

Then he turned from "The Bureau" and rushed on to seek
The settlers to eastward on Indian Creek:
The most of them listened to all that he said
And, deeply impressed by his message so dread,
To places of safety they hastily fled.
But one William Davis, a man of affairs,
With a millsite and farm and a shop for repairs,
Was impatient of warning, and said he would stay,
He had naught but contempt for such Indian play;
And he actually drove the old Chieftain away.

The messenger went, but quite soon he returned,
For though he and his message had been rudely spurned,
He was fully aware of the Indians' hate
And would fain save the man from a terrible fate;
But the proud pioneer remained obdurate.

Then the Chieftain, sad-hearted, proceeded again
On his course to the eastward to warn other men;
But the horse he was riding now slackened his speed,
He faltered and fell, for the spirited steed
Had run out his life to meet the great need.

Near a hundred miles he had kept to the pace
That had made a success of that wonderful race;
But the way was long, and he carried weight,
The fords were deep and the strain was great,—
He died in the doing, a glorious fate.

From his fallen horse, the gear Shabbona took
And, casting upon him a last grateful look,
He started on foot for the house of his friend,
George Hollenbeck, feeling he surely would lend
A fresh horse, that he might bring his work to an end.

He soon reached "The Grove," and as he had believed,
A welcome, a meal and a horse he received.
It was just thirty hours from the time he bestrode
His own steed, and set out from his humble abode,
Till to the last house with his warning he rode.

Great Shabbona said that he cared for no stone
To speak of his deeds when he should be gone;[140]
But some day in Ottawa, named for his race,
There shall stand 'neath the sky in a well-chosen place
An equestrian statue upon a fair base,

That shall show the great Chief on his foam-covered steed,
In his merciful race over valley and mead
To warn pioneers of the danger so great
And cause them to flee ere it should be too late,
That they might escape from a terrible fate.

THE EXPERIENCES OF MR. COMBS

May 15th

When the messenger came to the Harris home
    The husband and sons were away,
And the father-in-law, whose name was Combs,
    On a bed of suffering lay.

"O what shall I do, and my little ones?"
  Said the weeping daughter and wife;
And the father replied, "Take the little ones,
  And flee with them for your life.

"Do not be afraid to leave me alone:
  I am ready to meet my fate:
I am old and sick, and I can not live
  Very long at any rate."

So the poor distracted mother took
  Her little ones and fled,
Leaving her brave old father there
  Alone upon his bed.

In a little while the Indians came
  Their lust for blood to sate;
And finding the supper-table spread,
  They sat them down and ate.

As they took their fill they talked about
  Their intended victims' flight,
And they said, "We know it is Shabbona,
  Who has frightened our game to-night."

They found the suffering Mr. Combs,
  (These men of barbarous deeds,)
But instead of murdering him outright,
  They ministered to his needs.

They came to him daily for nearly a week,
  And brought to him food and drink:
For the chain that should bind all human hearts
  They had found the missing link.

Then a band of rangers came along
  On a bright and beautiful day:
Mr. Combs had then so much improved,
  He was able to ride away.

The Good Deed of Whiskey

May 15th

An Indian band raided Hollenbeck's store.
There plenty of whiskey they found,—it was more
To their liking just then than the prospects of gore,
And pursuit of the settlers they gladly forebore.

There was all that they wanted with nothing to pay.
They drank all the night, and throughout the next day
In the store and the store-yard they peacefully lay,
Giving settlers the chance for a good get-away.

Some Pottawatomies Join in the War

Some rash Pottawatomies joined in the war,
Their personal grievances reasons therefor,
The love of their race, surging up like a flood,
And the natural lust of the savage for blood.
Sometimes by themselves they made their attacks;
Sometimes they went out with war parties of Sacs.

The first and the foulest of deeds that they did
For thirty long years from white people was hid,
Till a son of the Chief, who that day had command,
Told the terrible tale of the work of the band.

The Rev. James Sample and Wife Burned at the Stake

May 16th

A preacher, James Sample, from Hennepin came
To the lands at Rock Island and laid out a claim,
Built a cabin and took to himself a fair wife,
In hopes there to dwell through a long, helpful life.

He was earnest and zealous and preached well the word,
And his soul-stirring message by many was heard.

In social relations the fair wife excelled,
And in highest esteem the young couple were held.

When the war-fearful settlers had heard the report
Of the coming of Black Hawk they fled to the fort.
The Samples grew restless as slow weeks went by,
And sold their possessions, determined to try
To get back to Hennepin, whence they had come
And there with old neighbors to set up a home.

On a beautiful morning the middle of May,
Well mounted and happy they started away,
Expecting to reach the West Bureau ere night;
At the door of H. Thomas, their friend, to alight;
But the lone door was closed, and no shelter was nigh:
They camped in a grove that was standing near by.

Next morning they forded the rain-swollen creek
And went to Smith's cabin, a welcome to seek;
But that too was closed and the people had gone,
As also from Epperson's place farther on.

As they left the last cabin their course to pursue,
A scene of great beauty was spread out to view.
With the grass of the spring the broad prairie was green,
While the brightest of flowers were growing between.
By the brooklets and creeks in full leaf were the trees,
And the fragrance of fruit blooms was borne on the breeze.
The squirrels were chat'tring, in song were the birds;
The joy of all nature was too great for words.

Sixty miles of their journey had been left behind,
Its end and the greeting of friends were in mind.
They were cantering slowly across the fair lands
Where the beautiful city of Princeton now stands,
With such hope in their hearts as left no room for fears,
When the war-whoop of savages burst on their ears.

'Twas the band of Mike Girty, the renegade's son,
The cruel half breed, the malevolent one.
They had called at each cabin with purposes dread;
But, warned by old Shabbona, settlers had fled.
Catching sight of the trav'lers they quickly gave chase,
In hopes to win scalps their war dances to grace.

But the high-mettled steeds that the travelers rode
Drew away from the ponies the Indians bestrode.
For a time they had hope to escape from the band,
But sad fate delivered them into their hand.

In a miry place Mrs. Sample's horse fell,
The red men came on with a deafening yell,
The preacher then drew forth his pistol and fired,
An Indian reeled from his horse and expired,
In a moment the blood-thirsty band gathered round,
The white couple were seized and with strong cords were
  bound.
A council condemned them to torture by fire,
With all its dread features till they should expire.[131]

Jefferson Davis Organizes a Regiment at Galena

Colonel Strode at Galena had been asked to raise
A force of militia within a few days;
But for leadership others began to contend,
And the Colonel concluded a message to send
To the General at Dixon's appealing for aid.
On the nineteenth of May his arrangements were made,
And a party of six started with the daylight.
They were ambushed by Indians before it was night,
And one of the men, William Durley, was slain,—
The others, well mounted, escaped o'er the plain.

General Atkinson, wishing to meet every need,
Sent Jefferson Davis and guard with all speed.

This officer, helped by the wise Captain Gear,
Soon enlisted a force to protect the frontier.

THE INDIAN CREEK MASSACRE

May 19th

One terrible deed that aroused all the land
Was done by a Sac-Pottawatomie band,
That was led on by Kee-was-see, burning to seek[132]
For revenge upon Davis of Indian Creek.

Other settlers were found at his cabin that day,
And a part of his debt each was called on to pay:
Men, women and children, they numbered a score;
Of these all were brutally slaughtered but four.[133]
Two young men escaped the dread tomahawk's blade,
And two maidens, the Hall girls, were prisoners made.

Jimmie Davis, aged seven, they took from the place,
But he was unable to keep up the pace
That was set by the riotous, blood-crazy band.
Two Indians in charge of him held each a hand:
Like a statue of marble he stood to be shot,
And the blood of a hero soon watered the spot.

THE CAPTIVITY AND RANSOM OF THE HALL GIRLS

Under charge of the Sauks of the party
    The Hall girls were taken away:
To the camp of the Black Hawk they journeyed,
    Ninety miles in a night and a day.

Their arrival caused greatest rejoicing:
    All the Indians gathered around,
Beating drums and whooping and yelling
    In a riotous discord of sound.

To the care of some squaws they were given,
   Who were with them by day and by night:
They gave them the kindest of treatment,
   But no chance was afforded for flight.

The Indians laid out a large circle,
   And carefully smoothed off the ground:
In the center a tall pole was planted,
   And spears were stuck up all around.

On the spears were the scalps of the murdered,
   Together with three human hearts:
The maidens were seated on blankets,
   For they too must play out their parts.

Fifty warriors, divested of clothing
   And with all of their faces made red,
Danced about them, yelling like demons,
   And flourishing war-clubs o'erhead.

This continued for nearly an hour,
   When suddenly there was a pause:
The maidens were raised from their blankets
   And returned to the care of the squaws.

Very soon they broke up the encampment
   And all in one body went forth,
Making way o'er a rough, barren prairie
   In the general direction of north.

．　．　．　．　．　．

General Atkinson through the sub-agent
   To rescue the prisoners sought,
And sent Whirling Thunder and White Crow
   To find out if they could be bought.

These men were the chief Winnebagoes,
  And both were well skilled in debate:
A council of Saukies was ordered
  To determine the prisoners' fate.

At full length the question was argued,
  Each phase of it duly was weighed;
And in spite of some strong opposition
  A bargain for ransom was made.[134]

Then a young Saukie brave who desired
  The beautiful Rachel as wife,
And had vowed he would keep her or kill her,
  Cut a lock from her hair with his knife,

And said to the old Winnebagoes:
  "It is well, you may go on your ways;
But take you good heed to my warning,—
  I will have her back here in three days."

Then another one, equally ardent
  In purpose a white girl to wed,
And with the same vow of persistence,
  Cut a lock from fair Sylvia's head.

The Chieftains, their men and the maidens
  Rode rapidly off through the night,
And reached their encampment in safety
  Before the return of the light.

On the third day they came to The Blue Mounds,
  And the Indians made their report
To the agent in charge, Colonel Gratiot,
  Who took the girls into the fort.

Improvised Forts and Irregular Rangers

As the news of the terrible massacre spread
From a wide stretch of country all settlers fled,
And gathered themselves to the few scattered forts
Or improvised others of various sorts.
One of these was Fort Beggs, which at Plainfield was made
Of fence-rails and logs as a rude barricade.

None too soon did they go, for the wide prairie lands
Were quickly o'errun by the Indian bands.
Against the marauders brave rangers were sent,
Who to rescue the settlers were also intent.

Captain Naper conducted the people away
From Fort Beggs to Chicago with little delay.
Captain Walker, commanding a few trusty men,
Went forth through the country again and again.
There were other like forces that ranged here and there,
The weak to defend and all dangers to dare.
On the nineteenth of June these roughriders were made
Buckmaster's battallion, not in a brigade.

The Murder of Adam Payne

May 23rd

Like Prophet in his prime
    Was Preacher Adam Payne.
His message waited not
    On any builded fane;
But here and there he went
    In forest or on plain,
To tell the truths of God
    As they to man pertain.

His long black hair and beard
    Had ne'er been touched by shears;
His sturdy, stalwart frame
    Felt not the weight of years;

His brave and kindly heart
    Knew naught of doubts or fears;
Upon his life's fair page
    There's naught but good appears.

Returning from the East,
    He stopped with Beggs one night:
The people who were there
    Were not prepared to fight,
And from the fort next day
    Were planning to take flight:
They plead with him to go
    With them at morning light.

He said he had no fears,
    He knew the Indians well,
He'd often gone to them,
    The gospel tale to tell:
If he could not escape,
    If to their hands he fell,
He thought in kindly ways
    He could their passions quell.

"In such a time as this
    It is my place to be
Wherever they are found
    With my own family.
I'm in the hands of God:
    He watches over me:
I'm safe with him in time
    Or in eternity."

When passing through a grove,
    Three Saukies who were there,
With rifles wounded him
    And killed his faithful mare.

With Bible in one hand
    And one raised as in prayer,
He asked the bloody men
    His peaceful life to spare.

Two Indians dropped their hands,
    The third with one great blow
The broad, white forehead crushed
    And laid the preacher low:
The others joined with him
    When blood began to flow,
And helped cut off his head
    As that of fallen foe.

One caught the long, black beard
    And o'er his shoulder slung
The ghastly, bleeding head:
    All to their ponies sprung,
And with the wildest speed
    Across the prairies swung
To take the news to camp,
    Where war songs must be sung.

COLONEL DODGE AND SUB-AGENT GRATIOT ON THE MINING FRONTIER

Before dawn on the day after Stillman's defeat,
    Colonel Dodge and his rangers set out
To make forts for all those on the mining frontier,
    In the settlements scattered about.

The work was soon done and the folks gathered in,
    Then Dodge with his company bold
And Sub-Agent Gratiot marched to Four Lakes,
    With the Indians a council to hold.

The sly Winnebagoes were asked to declare
    Just what they intended to do,
To take part with the Sacs or be friends to the whites,
    As this conflict was being fought through.

"The Saukies are liars," Dodge boldly affirmed,
    "And traitors: they want you to fight
For their cause; but when they shall have suffered defeat,
    They will seek their own safety in flight.

"They will use you as long as they think there is hope;
    But when all their efforts must cease,
They will leave you to suffer in blood and in tears,
    And in the hard terms of your peace."

So shrewd and so forceful were Gratiot and Dodge,
    That soon an arrangement was made
For all good Winnebagoes to quietly live,
    And not to the Sacs to give aid.

.   .   .   .   .   .

The two-faced Winnebagoes had wished to give aid
To Black Hawk and his band, but they were afraid
Of their Agents and Chieftains, and so they made claim
To be neutral, in hope to escape from all blame;
But doubtless they joined with the murdering bands,
In the blood of the settlers imbuing their hands.
They guided the Saukies as best they could do,
And misguided the soldiers as faithfully, too.

.   .   .   .   .   .

Small parties of Indians were roaming about
To pick off any white men who might venture out.
They scouted so well and so swiftly attacked,
That seldom a scalp for a trophy they lacked.
Near the mining frontier they slew nearly a score,
On the dead bodies sating their instincts for gore.

THE MURDER OF THE ST. VRAIN PARTY

May 24th

Mr. Felix de Lassus de Hault de St. Vrain
Was listed by Sauks as a man to be slain:
Their Agent he was and had been for some time;
But had counseled their going, which they thought a crime.

General Atkinson sent him with others to bear
To Fort Armstrong dispatches to those stationed there.
They got on very well till the second day out,
When the Indians attacked them and put them to rout.

Four men of the party were cruelly slain:
To the Indians' delight one of these was St. Vrain.
They cut off his head and his hands and his feet,
And, dividing his heart, they proceeded to eat.

Three others escaped by quick action in flight:
They hid in the daytime and traveled at night:
Through dangers they saw and did not see they passed,
Till they came to the town of Galena at last.

A FORWARD AND BACKWARD MOVEMENT
AND THE MUSTERING OUT OF
THE FIRST ARMY

On the nineteenth of May the whole army set forth
To pursue the Black Hawk, who had gone to the north.
To encourage the men General Atkinson went
With his aids,—also Reynolds with like good intent.

Colonels Taylor and Harney and other good men
From the regular troops, with militia again,
Marched along to assist, as there might be a need,
In making the force a great army, indeed.

As they pressed on with vigor the foemen to seek
An express brought the news from Indian Creek

Of the slaughter of innocents: Atkinson then
Returned to headquarters at Dixon's again,
Leaving Reynolds to do as might seem to him best
With the restless Militia in pushing the quest.

At a village abandoned by Indians they found
Some plunder and scalps that were cached in the ground.
From there on the trail was much harder to find,
The men were disheartened, and not much inclined
For further pursuit, their term had expired,
And to be at their homes they greatly desired.

A council of officers called to decide
What ought to be done, was seen to divide
In two equal parties. Whiteside in a pout
Said he only would lead them to be mustered out.

They marched to the south in a leisurely way,
And reached Ottawa upon the fourth day.
There they were discharged, but Atkinson then
Asked a short re-enlistment of one thousand men.

The Governor earnestly made an appeal,
In the name of a need that all must know was real.
Six companies, making a small regiment,
Were formed, and to guard the frontiers were sent.[135]

ANDREW JACKSON
President 1829-37

WILLIAM HENRY HARRISON
President 1841

ZACHARY TAYLOR
President 1849-50

ABRAHAM LINCOLN
President 1861-65

XVII. THE BLACK HAWK WAR, LATER STAGES

The March of Captain Iles' Company

June 5th to 16th

CAPTAIN ILES, on whose roll were the names of A.
    Lincoln,
J. D. Henry and other great men,
Was ordered to range o'er the land to Galena,
    And carefully range back again.

As Lieutenant Colonel had Henry been chosen,
    But as private continued to serve;
And acted as drill master, training the rangers
    The usage of war to observe.

This work that was needed, so well was accomplished,
    That be it by day or by night,
He had but to sound forth a call, and the rangers
    Sprang into their places for fight.

In due time the troopers arrived at Galena;
    Next morning they turned them about
And marched back to Dixon's, from thence to Fort Wilburn
    And on the sixteenth mustered out.

Captain Snyder's Battle at Burr Oak Grove[136]

June 16th

Kellogg's Grove was a place of strategic importance
    In the wandering war of that day:
'Twixt the ferry at Dixon's and mines at Galena
    Its position was nearly half way.

Captain Snyder was sent out with sixty-nine troopers
    To this grove, known as "Kellogg's Old Place."
Major Riley attended with regular soldiers:
    They were there to establish a base.

On the night of the fifteenth their troops were well quartered
    And the sentinels posted about
In every direction. 'Twas dark as a pocket
    Save when the bright lightning flashed out.

A listening guard heard an Indian breathing,
    As he stood at his post by a tree.
He peered through the darkness in vain to discern him,
    When a flash of the lightning showed three.

He grappled with one and was able to throw him,
    And run in with a cry of alarm.
The Indians pursued him and shot through the darkness,
    But the sentry escaped without harm.

The camp was aroused: they called in the sentries
    And lay on their arms through the night;
Then the volunteer troop under brave Captain Snyder
    Sallied forth at the breaking of light.

They soon struck the trail of a band of the Indians,
    And coming upon them killed four:
One man of the troopers was mortally wounded,
    And from further pursuit they forbore.

As toward Kellogg's Grove they were slowly retiring
    A large band of Indians engaged:
In numbers they equaled the force of the troopers,
    And a very hot battle was waged.

But both sides found shelter behind trees and bushes;
    Fatalities therefore were few:
Two troopers were slain, and the Chief of the Indians,
    And then the red forces withdrew.

The Battle of "The Pecatonica"

June 16th

Four murders near Hamilton Fort
    Performed by an Indian band
Called aloud for a punishment dire:
    Colonel Dodge and his troop were at hand.

A small party, detached from the force,
    To bury the bodies was sent,
While the Colonel with twenty-nine men
    In pursuit of the murderers went.

Well guided they soon struck the trail
    Of those they had come out to seek:
Through the swamps and the woods it led down
    To the big Pecatonica Creek.

The Indians were hid 'neath the bank,
    That arose from the edge of the lake,
Where they hoped when the foe should approach
    The best of resistance to make.

From their place of concealment they fired,
    And in death two troopers were laid:
Colonel Dodge then ordered a charge,
    And the order was promptly obeyed.

The soldiers rushed on to the bank
    And poured down a volley like rain
On the Indians lurking below,
    Of whom eleven were slain.

Two others plunged into the lake,
    But were shot before they had crossed:
Thus the lives of the bloody thirteen
    In their turn through blood-shedding were lost.[137]

The Battle of Prairie Grove

June 18th

Captain Stephenson ranged the Galena frontier:
He was constant in action and never knew fear.
One day he discovered a small Saukie band
That fled to a thicket and there made a stand.
He attacked them at once with his twenty-one men,
And charged through the thicket again and again.
Three troopers were slain and an Indian, too,
The Captain was hurt, and his forces withdrew.

The Killing of Elijah Phillips

June 17th

As time passed away in the forts and stockades
Without any news of more Indian raids,
A few of the bold and adventurous men
In small parties went back to their cabins again,
To look after stock that had been left to roam
And to bring to their people some comforts from home.

A party of seven from Hennepin went
About twenty miles north to the home of Ament.
They made fast the cabin and there spent the night.
One Phillips went out with the coming of light,

But was shot by the Indians lurking near by,
Who then sprang to the door with a terrible cry:
In an instant 'twas barred, and the settlers all
Soon were firing their guns through the chinks in the wall.

Ziba Dimmick was only a lad of fifteen,
But as fine a young horsemen as ever was seen:
He called to the window his pony, named Jack,
Made a leap and alighted astride of his back,
And then without saddle or bridle or rein,

Like the wind in a frolic he swept o'er the plain
Twenty miles to old Hennepin, where help was found.
A brave band of rangers were soon on the ground:
Observing their coming, the Indians fled,
The settlers were saved, and the scalp of the dead.

THE SLAUGHTER OF MESSRS. SCHERMERHORN AND HAZELTON

June 24th

Northeast from Fort Johnson some rangers were sent:
In their wake with a wagon two settlers went:
The Indians concealed in the thickets and grass,
Permitted the rangers in safety to pass,
But fell on the settlers with hatchets and knives,
And in Indian fashion soon ended their lives.

A ranger, delayed, who chanced to be near,
Was attacked by an Indian, bearing a spear;
But his horse was fleet, and he rode him well,
And escaped to the fort the sad story to tell.

THE KILLING OF JAMES BERESFORD

The very same day a small party went out
Along the west side of Fox River to scout:
A shot from the thicket laid one of them low
And wounded the horse of another, although
The brave beast with his rider toward Ottawa sped
Far away from all danger before he fell dead.

THE ORGANIZATION OF THE NEW ARMY

The Governor went to the settlements
To encourage enlistments for coming events.
By the fifteenth of June over three thousand men
Had gathered to hunt for the Black Hawk again.

By changes in plan the place of resort
For enlistment by these had been fixed at a fort
Called Wilbourn, about twenty miles below
Ottawa, as a bird through the air might go.

The army was formed into three brigades,
With sev'ral battallions as scouters and aids.[138]
Some rangers besides and the Michigan corps
Of General Dodge made a full thousand more.

The three Brigadiers were well chosen men,
Alexander and Posey and Henry, and when
They were put to the test in the wild northern land
They fully made proof of their right to command.

General Atkinson promptly to Fort Dixon sent
A battalion commanded by Colonel Dement
To report to Z. Taylor, the Commandant there,
And take orders from him to go anywhere.

The army soon followed, for Atkinson's plan
In all its details from Dixon's began.
There was hope in the air: commanders and men
Felt sure that good fortune was coming again.

BLACK HAWK ATTACKS APPLE RIVER FORT

June 24th

Meanwhile the Black Hawk with pappooses and squaws
    And the Winnebagoes to guide,
Had made his way up toward the Rock River's source,
    In the swamps and the marshes to hide.

Provisions were scanty, but from time to time
    Small parties sent out would arrive
With food of some sort, and in quantities, too,
    Sufficient to keep them alive.

With his medicine bag and two hundred men
  The Black Hawk started out for a raid,
The first it would seem, with so large a force,
  That he or his warriors had made.

He went to the west, and the second night out
  He dreamed that as forward he led,
On another day's travel, his warriors and braves,
  Before them a feast there was spread.

He told them the dream at the coming of dawn,
  And shortly they started away
For Mos-o-cho-coy-nak, the Apple Creek Fort,
  Which they reached in the heat of the day.

An express on the road to Dixon's came by,
  As they lay in the bushes and grass:
'Twas made up of four men, and the chance was too good
  For an Indian band to let pass.

A volley was sent and the man in the lead
  Appeared to be wounded and fell;
But he waved his right hand, and the other three men
  Looked backward and set up a yell.

The Indians fearing the troops were at hand,
  (According to Black Hawk's report,)
Remained quiet, and thus gave the white men a chance
  To rush on and enter the fort.

In a short time the Indians moved to attack,
  And a venturesome white man fell dead;
But the others defending shot out through the chinks,
  While the women made bullets of lead.

The contest continued for two or three hours,
  When the Black Hawk naively said:
"Our only way is to fire the fort,
  If we wish to make these people dead.

"But to light such a blaze a signal might be
    For the army to come in great force,
And spoil all our plans, so that the result
    For us in the end would be worse.

"Provisions and cattle and horses we need
    Let us take all of these we can find:
They will make better food than the white people's scalps,—
    At least it seems so to my mind."

So said and so done: they opened the stores,
    Filled their bags, and at close of the day
With horses and cattle that they cared to take,
    They joyfully went on their way.

With the coming of darkness a messenger sped
    To Galena, some twelve miles away,
Colonel Strode was informed and rapidly came
    With a troop on the following day.

THE BATTLE OF KELLOGG'S GROVE

June 25th

On June twenty-second Colonel Dement,
    With a hundred and fifty men,
Arrived at Dixon's: the very next day
    At dawn, he departed again,

Under orders from Taylor to go to the fort
    At Kellogg's Grove, and to hold
It against an attack that might be made
    By the Saukie warriors bold.

On the evening of the twenty-fourth,
    Isaac Funk stopped to tell of the band,[139]
That had made an attack on the Apple Creek Fort,
    And would doubtless soon be at hand.

The brave and capable Colonel Dement,
   A conference held in the night,
And plans were laid in a soldierly way
   For carrying on the fight.

The Colonel, alert, with the coming of dawn
   A well chosen party sent out,
To reconnoiter and make a report
   If Indians were lurking about.

As they carefully scouted they saw three or four,
   And sent an express back to tell:
The soldiers, not waiting for orders, dashed forth
   In a wild, reckless fashion, pell mell.

The Indian decoys very quickly gave way;
   The soldiers rushed on to a dell;
Black Hawk and his warriors, firing their guns,
   Sprang out with a terrible yell.

The soldiers, who recklessly rode to the fight
   When the enemy numbered but four,
Now turned them about in inglorious flight,
   In the face of two hundred or more.

Dement, who vainly had tried to restrain
   The soldiers, now made a brave stand,
With a few kindred spirits of true martial type,
   'Gainst the rush of the on-coming band.

But the odds were too great, they were forced to give way
   Before the Black Hawk in his might.
They fired a volley, and turned from the field
   To seek their own safety in flight.

The fort was secure, though the Indians tried
   To reach it with long distance fire.
They shot forty horses scattered about,
   And then were content to retire,

15

For the old Black Hawk sententiously said:
    "To his hole we have run the bear.
We can not dig him out, and 'tis no use to try,
    It is better to leave him there."

Five men, well mounted, had early been sent
    To Dixon's to tell of the fight.
They had made good time, and Posey's brigade
    Was at Kellogg's before it was night.

Next morning the General attempted pursuit,
    But the Saukies had scattered,—their trail
Was not to be followed, and Posey well knew
    That to try would be but to fail.

LIGHT VERSE ON A SERIOUS SUBJECT

1831

Black Buffalo loved a good horse,
    So he swapped with a white man one day;
But the horse hated Indian ways,
    And, taking a chance, slipped away.

When the Indians all flew the coop,
    And hastily crossed the big creek,
Black Buffalo lingered behind
    In order his charger to seek.

The troops coming out from the fort,
    No sooner had gotten to land,
Than they spied this same Black Buffalo
    On his way, with a bridle in hand.

Major Bliss called on Spencer to ask,
    Where the rest of the band could be found.
Black Buffalo blandly replied,
    They were all on the Iowa ground.

The Major told Spencer to say
　To the man, he would kill him forsooth,
If, regarding the matter in hand,
　He told anything else than the truth.

Again with a blandness supreme,
　The Indian proceeded to say,
It was only the truth that he spoke:
　He was sent to the fort for the day.

1832

On the night after Stillman's defeat,
　The horse of the Black Buffalo
Galloped into the old Dixon town,
　Making proof that he wasn't so slow.

．　．　．　．　．　．

When the Kellogg's Grove battle was fought,
　The whites made retreat to the fort,
But the horses were tethered outside,
　And were targets for Indian sport.

One horse was observed to go off,
　In a strange, halting way, while the grass
In front of him wavered and shook,
　As though something was trying to pass.

At the wiggle a few shots were sent,
　And when they went out to the place,
A dead Indian lay in the grass,
　Who bore the Black Buffalo's face.

XVIII. THE BLACK HAWK WAR, CLOSING EVENTS

THE SECOND ARMY MOVES AFTER BLACK HAWK

GENERAL Atkinson planned a forceful campaign:
  At Dixon's a troop was detached to remain,
Then Posey to Hamilton Fort was sent,
As also the valorous Major Dement;
The brave Alexander was ordered to go
To the westward to check the flight of the foe,
While the General himself and Henry set forth
In search of the Black Hawk, away to the north,—
There was also a small Pottawatomie band,[140]
Waubonsie and Shabbona, Chiefs in command.

It was June the eighth and twentieth day
When Atkinson's forces started away
From Dixon's, their course up the river to take,—
On the third of July they reached Koshkonong Lake.

On the fourth, Alexander, no foe having found,
As ordered, came on to his chief's camping ground.
Its course to Burnt Village the army now made:
Dodge's troop there joined them, and Posey's brigade.

Scouting parties went out, but no sign of the foe
Could be found.   Days passed and provisions were low.
On the tenth some detachments to Dixon's were sent:
Early's troop was dicharged, and with these forces went.[141]

General Posey's brigade of resolute men
Was ordered to Hamilton Fort again.
Alexander and Henry and Dodge were sent forth
To Fort Winnebago, northwestward by north,
For supplies.   They were charged not to stay very long,

But to quickly return to Lake Koshkonong.
While waiting for those he'd sent out to report,
Atkinson, falling back to the lake, built a fort.

The Advance of Henry and Dodge and the Battle of Wisconsin Heights

Alexander and Henry and Dodge
   Went swiftly upon their way,
And reached Winnebago Fort
   At evening upon the third day.

They were weary and soon pitched their tents,
   While the horses were loosed on the mead:
Some Indians, as has been supposed,
   Disturbed them and caused a stampede.

They rushed through the camp with great force
   Razing tents and bruising the men:
When they came to the river they turned[142]
   And as wildly they dashed back again.

The result was nearly as bad
   As the charge of a troop might have been,
And it took a large part of next day
   The horses to find and bring in.

When they were about to return,
   Winnebagoes brought a report
That the Sauks on Rock River were camped,
   About fifty miles east of the fort.

An officers' council was called,
   Which considered it best to transcend
General Atkinson's orders, in hope
   Of bringing the war to an end.

Alexander was loath to concur,
    And when he consulted his men,
Concluded his honor required
    That he quickly should go back again.

Major Dodge's battalion was small,
    And of horses there was a great lack:
He was eager to seek for the foe,
    But more prudent it seemed to go back.

Disaffection reached Henry's brigade,
    And some to return were inclined:
A remonstrance was drawn up at length,
    Which a few of the officers signed.

But Henry was born to command,
    And the courage to do so possessed:
He ordered each man who had signed
    To be put at once under arrest,

And sent back to Atkinson's camp
    To be tried and perhaps to be shot:
This humbled the bold mutineers,
    And for pardon they begged on the spot.

From Galena fresh horses arrived,
    And July fifteenth was the day
That Henry and Dodge started forth
    Their self-chosen task to essay.

On the eighteenth Rock River they reached.
    The guides, with a treacherous mind,
Told them they must go up the stream
    In order the Saukies to find.

Then Henry to Atkinson sent
    An express to tell him of their quest:
They had gone eight miles when they struck
    The trail of the Sauks leading west.

It was evening. They stopped to make sure
   By the aid of the fast failing light,
And then hastened back to the camp
   In the gloom of the gathering night.

The report that was brought by these men
   Served the march-weary troops to enthuse.
Next morning the faithful express
   Sought Atkinson's camp with the news.

The troops were as one in desire
   Very early their march to renew:
Camp baggage was all left behind,
   That the foe they might quickly pursue.

The first night out they were caught
   In a terrible downpour of rain,
With no tents to cover their heads;
   But no one was heard to complain.

The second night out they encamped
   On the eastern shore of Third Lake,
And there for the first time prepared
   Substantial refreshments to take.

Bright and early July twenty-first
   They continued pursuit with great zest;
And from baggage thrown out by the way
   They knew that the foe was hard pressed.

The Black Hawk kept out a rear guard,
   Who feinted and welcomed attack,
But when the white forces were formed
   Gave way before them and fell back.

This they did again and again,
   Till at length the old Chief with his band
Formed lines in a well chosen place,
   With the purpose of making a stand,

Till the women and children could pass
    O'er the river, or such as should choose
Might prepare to float down its tide
    In quickly constructed canoes.[143]

General Henry arranged his command,
    With soldierly care for the fight:
Collins left, Jones center and Dodge
    With his Michigan rangers at right.

Major Ewing was sent to the front
    To draw out the enemy's fire,
While Fry was held in reserve
    To be used as need might require.

As Ewing and Collins and Jones
    Pressed forward, the Saukies broke rank
And fell to their left before Dodge,
    Attempting to turn on his flank.

Colonel Fry from his place in reserve
    Was quickly sent forward to aid,
And, having come up, on the Sauks,
    A vigorous onset was made.

Before this the Indians fell back,
    From a better position to fight:
They were there charged upon and dispersed
    By the troops that now came from their right.

From the bluffs to the bottom below,
    Through the grass and the timber they fled:
They had held the white forces in check,
    But at heavy expense in their dead.[144]

The darkness came on and the whites
    Encamped where they were till the day;
But the Saukies crossed over the flood
    And toilsomely went on their way.[145]

Next morning Henry advanced
  To the river. No Saukies were found;[146]
And, being in need of supplies,
  He marched to the fort at Blue Mound.

There Atkinson's force had arrived:
  All troops were united, and when
Provisions had been taken on,
  The army moved forward again.

BLACK HAWK SPEAKS OF NAHPOPE

Black Hawk states that as they journeyed
Toward the broad Wisconsin River,
Nahpope with some twenty warriors
In the rear watched for the army.

When the fight was on these warriors
Were not to be seen, and Black Hawk
Says that he was much astonished.

It appears they missed the army,
And that Nahpope and one other,
Thinking only of their safety
Sought a Winnebago village.

But the others, being brave men,
Mindful of a warriors duty,
Later joined the fleeing Saukies.

ATKINSON'S PURSUIT AND THE BATTLE
OF THE BAD AXE

General Atkinson's army marched from the Blue Mound
July twenty-fifth. In three days they found
The trail of the enemy, leading north-west,
And as fast as they could they pushed on in their quest.

The order of march was: the scouts in advance,
Then the regular troops,—they must have their chance,
Alexander and Posey, without fault or fear,
And Henry, in charge of supplies, in the rear.

The way led through a rough, almost mountainous land,
Sometimes by the swamps and sometimes over sand.
Through timber and thickets and vines they must go,
And it only could be that their progress was slow.

As they followed the trail, the pitifulness
Of those they pursued, their want and distress,
Touched the hearts of the soldiers with sympathy for
A people 'gainst whom they had come out to war.

It appeared that the Indians had nothing to eat,[147]
But the ponies that died, or were killed for their meat:
The trail was well marked by the things thrown away,
And at every encampment the brown corpses lay.

On August the first the wretched Sauk band,
Worn down by the toils of their march over land,
Reached the great river's side by the Bad Axe's mouth,
As a steamboat, The Warrior, was just going south.

Black Hawk knew the captain,—a white flag he brought,
And under its folds a conference sought;
But the Captain made answer with powder and ball,
And reported he saw twenty Indians fall.

Farther sport of that kind he was forced to forego
For his fuel gave out, and he dropped down below.
The old Chieftain then bade farewell to his band,
And started away for the Chippewa land.

Next morning at daybreak a young warrior bold,
And fleet as a deer, overtook him and told
That all of the Saukies were planning to cross;
But that white men were near and they feared a great loss.

Thus appealed to the Black Hawk decided to go
And do what he could to withstand the great foe.
Having made up his mind, very quickly he sped
With his brave back to camp, and undoubtedly led
The red men who decoyed the General away
From the main band of Saukies on that fateful day.[148]

It was August the second when Atkinson's force
Reached the bluffs, as onward they sped in their course.
The hour was near noon, and the Black Hawk was then
Concealed in the brush with about twenty men.

He feinted attack and drew Atkinson's fire,
And so he continued to feint and retire
As the army pursued, and drew it away
From the camp where the body of Indians lay.

When Henry came up he was quick to perceive,
That Black Hawk had enticed the army to leave
The broad Saukie trail. Without orders to go
He quickly passed down to the valley below.

Deploying his men, he detached and sent out
A small band to pass toward the river and scout.
They boldly advanced, but not far had they gone
Till a fire they drew, and the battle was on.

'Twas a desperate fight, but the Saukies gave way,
And the rangers pursued over corpses that lay
Like leaves on the ground. The bugles blew, "Charge,"
And the remnant was forced to the great river's marge.
At the bayonet's point some fell down to die,
While others escaped to an island near by.

Just then Atkinson arrived on the scene,
And to take a small part all his forces were keen.
Under orders to which they were glad to respond,
They waded or swam to the island beyond,

And captured or killed all the Sauks who were there,
Save a few, who midway between hope and despair,
Plunged into the Father of Waters so wide,
To battle for life with its onflowing tide;
But the steamboat, The Warrior, had come back and lay
In their course to take toll on that terrible day.

Few indeed were the remnants of that wretched band,
Who escaped from the fight to the Iowa land,
Though some, who had crossed on the evening before
And some in the morning, were safe on that shore.[149]
Black Hawk and the band of defenders he led,
When they knew all was lost, to the wilderness fled.[150]

. . . . . .

As Lieutenant Anderson went from the field[151]
He heard the low moan of a pappoose, concealed
'Neath the corpse of a squaw, who had fallen that day.
He rescued the girl and bore her away
To the surgeon, for that which had done fatal harm
To the mother had wounded the child in the arm.
Amputation was needed. The old doctor said,
"As I work let her gnaw on a hard piece of bread."
So they did, and the little one made not a moan
As he cut through the flesh and sawed off the bone.

. . . . . .

A squaw by the onrushing tide undismayed,
With her child on her shoulders, a crossing essayed.
She boldly struck out, but seemed certain to fail
Till a pony came by,—she caught hold of its tail,
And safely was towed through the waters so wide,
Far away from the fight to the Iowa side.[152]

General Scott Sent to Take Command

The President, impatient of delays
(Which he ascribed to dilatory ways

Upon the part of those called on to lead,)
With purpose to secure a greater speed,
Sent General Winfield Scott to take command[153]
And push the war against the Saukie band.

He had six hundred men or thereabout,
And on the lakes the cholera broke out.
He reached Chicago on the very day
That Henry from Burnt Village went away:
There with his stricken troops long days he spent,
And then with two or three to Dixon's went,
Arriving there upon the self-same day
That saw the Sauks' defeat in awful fray.

Thence on he pushed, with little rest I ween,
And on the seventh came to old du Chien.
There, as Commander, first his name appears
On orders for discharge of volunteers.
He then directed that his troops be sent
To Rocky Island, whence he also went,
While Atkinson and his Command fell down
To their own barracks near Saint Louis town.

On August twenty-sixth, as had been feared,
The dreaded cholera again appeared:
The General nursed his men from day to day,
And though some died, he drove the scourge away.

General Street Sends the Winnebago Chiefs After Black Hawk and Winneshiek

General Street, the agent at Prairie du Chien,
As able a man as appeared on the scene,
Had charge of the prisoners, and he was told
Black Hawk and the Prophet to capture and hold.

He called in his Chiefs and said he would know
If they wished to be friends or be classed with the foe.
If friends he desired that they should go forth,
To take Hawk and Prophet, who'd gone to the north,
And bring them to him just as soon as they could,—
Such an act on their part would speak well for their good.
It was August the seven and twentieth day
That they brought in the men with excuse for delay.

Address of the One-Eyed Decori to General Street on Delivering Black Hawk and the Prophet

My Father, I now stand before you,
　　With the two that you sent us to get:
We have traveled a very long distance,—
　　'Twas a difficult task that you set.

But we always do what you tell us,
　　For we know that it is for our good:
You said it would help Winnebagoes,
　　And we did it as quick as we could.

You told us to bring them here living,
　　'Twas the men still alive that you sought:
If their heads you had asked us to bring you,
　　Then only their heads we'd have brought.

To your hands these men we deliver:
　　Our friend we believe you to be:
If it must be that they shall be injured,
　　Their hurting we wish not to see.

Little birds have been flying about us:
　　They told us we'd suffer some day,
That evil would reach Winnebagoes:
　　We hope they'll be driven away.

You say that you love your red children,
　　And we feel very sure that you do,
You have taken our part and we trust you;
　　But we think that much more we love you.

We have come in great haste and are weary:
  We now put these men into your hands:
We hope you'll do much for our people,
  For we have fulfilled your commands.

CHAETER'S REPORT TO GENERAL STREET

I am neither a chief nor a speaker,
  But I heard what you said t'other day:
Into ear, brain and heart your word entered;
  That same night I went forth on my way.

You said if Black Hawk and the Prophet
  Should as captives be brought to you here,
No cloud would hang o'er Winnebagoes,
  But their skies would forever be clear.

I have been a great way and had trouble,
  But I know that you said what was right:
I did this for the good of my nation,
  And I hope future years will be bright.

It was I and none other, 'twas Chaeter,
  Who took the Black Hawk at the dalles:
I say this in the ears of all present,—
  They will know it till memory fails.

To our grandfather, to the Great Spirit,
  Who all things holds under his sway,
And to the great Earth, our grandmother,
  I appeal: 'tis the truth that I say.

This one, who is known as the Prophet,
  Is somewhat related to me:
If it must be that he shall be injured,
  His hurting I wish not to see.

General Street's Address to the Winnebagoes

My children, you have done well,
  You have done what I told you to do:
I am pleased at what you have done,
  It will certainly be good for you.

I assured the great warrior Chief,
  If these men in your country should be,
You would do the one thing that he wished,
  You would find them and bring them to me.

I can now do much for your good:
  To Rock Island I'll go with these men:
I wish you, who have brought them to me,
  To go also with others and then

You will counsel with General Scott,
  The War Chieftain who has been sent,
With the Governor of Illinois,
  That together they might represent

The Great Father in Washington.
  This remains for the tribe now to do:
To send also wise warriors and chiefs.
  In three days I will go down with you.

Winnebagoes who live to the south
  And some from my agency here
Have been giving aid to the Sauks:
  Such conduct has done harm, I fear.

I am pleased that you've taken these men,
  It will tend to your nation's relief:
It will help me to say much for you
  To your Father and to the Great Chief.

Colonel Taylor's in charge at the fort,
　And it is the Great Chieftain's command
That the prisoners, whom you have brought,
　I shall now give into his hand.

COLONEL TAYLOR'S REMARKS ON ACCEPTING THE PRISONERS

As the Great Chieftain said I should do,
　I will keep the men safe, and will treat
Them with kindness and send them to him,
　When you go down with General Street.

The Great Chief will take them in his care,
　And treat them in every respect
As the Father in Washington,
　Himself, shall see fit to direct.

ADDRESS SAID TO HAVE BEEN DELIVERED BY BLACK HAWK TO GENERAL STREET WHEN BROUGHT IN A PRISONER BY THE WINNEBAGOES

Your prisoner I now am here.
The cause is lost I held so dear.
I fought you hard.　Though in retreat,
I did not soon expect defeat.
Your bullets flew like birds in air,
Or like the wind through branches bare.

Around me fell my warrior band.
I saw my evil day at hand.
The sun rose with no threat'nings dire.
It sank in clouds, a ball of fire.
It was the last sun that ere shone
On Black Hawk.　All his hopes are gone.
He now is in the white man's hand,
But well the torture he can stand.
He has no fear of coming death.
He never drew a coward's breath.

An Indian true he takes no blame.
Naught has he done to cause him shame.
For his own people he has fought
Against the white men, who have sought
Each year to cheat the Indian bands
And to despoil them of their lands.

You know the reason for the war.
All white men know the cause therefor.
They ought to be ashamed of it,
And all their wrongs 'gainst us admit.
The whites despise the Indian bands
And drive them from their homes and lands;
But Indians speak out what they feel,
They're not deceitful, do not steal.

The Black Hawk is well satisfied.
He's done his duty, and with pride
Into the spirit world he'll go.
His father'll meet him and bestow
Upon him merited reward,
And all will praise with one accord.

The white men do not scalp the head,
But worse, they poison hearts instead.
Although from us no scalps they'll take,
Like to themselves our folks they'll make,
And in our towns there must be then
As many officers as men
To care for us and keep us straight.
For a free Indian what a fate!
Farewell then to my tribe, the Sauk!
Farewell then also to Black Hawk!

The Prisoners Are Taken to Jefferson Barracks

When a few days had passed "The Warrior" went down
  With the prisoners under the care
Of Jefferson Davis, who during the war
  As Lieutenant had done his full share.

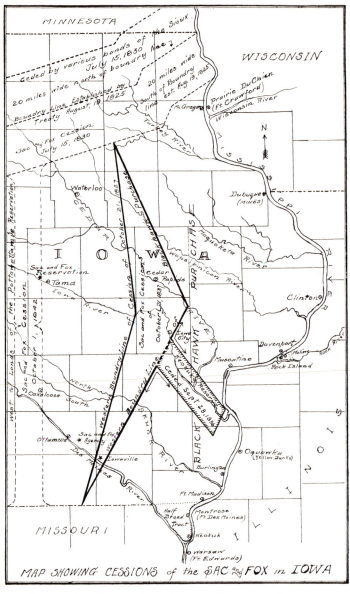

MAP SHOWING CESSIONS of the SAC and FOX in IOWA

MAP OF EAST PART OF IOWA SHOWING CESSIONS OF LAND BY
SACS AND FOXES
Drawn by Ben H. Wilson

The cholera raged at Rock Island, and Scott
  Sent them on to "The Barracks", to wait[154]
As Atkinson's captives, until the time came
  When the dreadful disease should abate.

But there they were held through the long, weary months;[155]
  Then in spring they were sent to the east:
After having been shown the full strength of the whites,
  They were brought back again and released.

A Treaty of Peace and Cession[156]

After war there must come a peace treaty,
  And those who have lost in the fight
Must consent to such terms as the winners
  May say that they think to be right.

The band of Black Hawk was a faction
  Unrestrained by the rest of the tribe,
To which as responsible party
  His deeds did the nation ascribe.

As always, the white men considered
  The Sacs and the Foxes as one;
And the latter were held with the former,
  Though they scarcely had fired a gun.

The treaty completed made cession
  Of lands about fifty miles wide,
In the beautiful Iowa country,
  That boarders the great river's side.

Twenty thousand a year in hard money,
  By the nation was pledged to be made,
And provision for widows and orphans
  Of Sacs slain in battle was made.

Scott and Reynolds were duly appointed,
  For the nation their names to subscribe:
Nine Saukies and twenty-four Foxes
  Made marks on behalf of the tribe.

XIX. THE EASTERN TRIP AND THE RETURN

Keokuk and Others Visit Black Hawk
at the Barracks

KEOKUK and some others, as spring-time drew near[157]
Went down to "The Barracks", the Black Hawk to
cheer,
Bringing with them his well beloved daughter and wife,
Who best could beguile him from thoughts of his strife.

The Head Man and his Chiefs sought the old man's release,
And gave every pledge for his conduct in peace;
But it had been decided the captives should go
To Washington, thence to the Fortress Monroe.

Black Hawk and His Fellow Prisoners
Taken to Washington

When spring-time came and Nature sprang again to active
life,
And soldiers turned to peaceful paths, forgetting bloody
strife,
Black Hawk and fellow prisoners to Washington was sent,
And with them as invited guests some other Saukies went.[158]
There General Jackson greeted them with kindly words and
grave:
Black Hawk responded with a speech, as Saukie Chief and
Brave.

Black Hawk Addresses the President

I am a man, and you are another.
I stand as your prisoner here;
But though I have been defeated in battle,
I do not tremble nor fear.

I took up the hatchet, as should the avenger
  Of wrongs that could not be endured:
I did not expect to defeat the white forces,
  But I fought that our rights be secured.

Had I borne any longer these wrongs without striking,
  They'd have said, "The Black Hawk is no Sac,"
So I sounded the war whoop and gathered my people,
  Determined as struck to strike back.

I need not speak further,—you know the whole matter,
  Concerning myself and my band:
When Keokuk came, you gave him a welcome
  And in friendship took him by the hand.

When he wished to return to his home and his people,
  You were willing for him so to do:
What you did for this Chieftain, when he made his visit,
  We hope you will do for us too.

The Prisoners Sent to Fortress Monroe and Later Released

The President attended, then Black Hawk's request declined
And sent the men to Fort Monroe for weeks to be confined.
One Colonel Eustis was in charge, who gave them kindly
  care,
Till they were sent to Baltimore, to meet with Jackson
  there.[159]
The President made an address and gave them their release,
Upon the pledges of their Chiefs that they would dwell in
  peace.

Address of President Jackson to the Prisoners

When I saw you in Washington, I told you that last year
You very badly had behaved out on the west frontier,
In taking up the tomahawk against white people there,
And killing men and women too, and little children fair.
Such conduct by your forces made it necessary for
Me to send many soldiers out and carry on a war.

You were defeated with great loss, and now as leaders here
Are prisoners within my hands till it shall be made clear,
That if returned to home and friends you will not cause alarm
Among white people, or to them do any deed of harm.

The Generals have sent me word that Keokuk, Head Chief,
And all your people wish that I should grant to you relief,
While Keokuk, himself, when here asked me for your
    release,
And with his Chiefs gave me a pledge that you would live
    in peace.
I'm satisfied you'll not again lead forth a hostile band,
And by my orders you will be sent back to your own land.

Our Major Garland, now with you, your friend and guide
    will be:
He'll take you through some of our towns, where you can
    plainly see
How numerous our people are. 'Gainst us what can you do?
Some of our women you may kill, and tender children, too,
But such a force of our young men against you we would
    send,
As very speedily would bring your whole tribe to an end.

Let red men care for their loved ones within their tribes
    and bands,
But 'gainst their brethren of the whites let them not raise
    their hands.
We've no desire to injure you, we wish for you the best,
But should you plunge your knife again into the white man's
    breast,
I will against you send a force, that will not ask for ease
Till they have fully punished you for all your cruelties.

When you return attend to counsels Keokuk shall give,
The tomahawk put by, and as a friendly Indian live;

And may the Spirit, Great and Good, who cares for all
  below,
Give you fair skies, and smooth the path before you as
  you go.

BLACK HAWK'S REPLY

My Father, I have heard your words,
  And have been glad to hear:
I shall be happy to return
  To home and kindred dear.

Last summer I did not behave,—
  All that I feel and know:
The hatchet I should not have raised
  To strike an angry blow;

But all my folks had suffered much,—
  (We will leave that behind,)
When I get back the words you speak,
  Shall be fixed in my mind.

I will not go to war again,
  But I will live in peace;
And as I hold you by the hand,
  Our friendship shall not cease.

THE CIRCUITOUS JOURNEY HOME

Much impressed had the prisoners been as they journeyed
From Jefferson Barracks to Washington City;
At first by the boat up "The Beautiful River,"
Past Louisville town and the great Cincinnati,
Till at length they arrived at the good town of Wheeling.

Thence by stage coach they passed over roads well con-
  structed
Through a rocky and rough and mountainous country,
Then down through a plain until, wonder of wonders!

They came by and by to the B. & O. Railroad,
Where coaches were taken along very swiftly
By the power of steam, as are boats on the river.

At Washington City they saw the great chamber,
Where in council assemble the Chiefs of the Nation,
The Great Father's mansion, substantial and pretty,
The arsenal, too, where the great guns were resting.

Everywhere that they went they were treated with kindness,
And especially so, as it seemed, by the women.
Even when by the orders the Father had given
They were held for a time within walls of a fortress,
They received the most kindly and generous treatment.

When taken in charge by their guide, Major Garland,
By steamboat they went to the great "Quaker City."
They were shown there the mint, where medals and money
Were made, and received many pieces as presents.
They also observed the white troops in maneuvers,
Which so moved the Black Hawk that thus he addressed
   them:

"I loved my own people, my village and country:
The white men encroached, and my hot heart grew bitter;
My hands were made strong, and I dug up the hatchet;
I led on my warriors, and I was no coward;
Much rich blood was shed, but the white men were mighty;
And they were as many as leaves of the forest;
The result, as you know, was that we were defeated,
And in barracks and fortress I have been a captive.

"The strength of the white men I freely acknowledge:
The Indians are few, but they are not cowards.
While the Great Spirit keeps my heart as at present,
In peace I will live, and with white men be friendly.
Now that I'm permitted, I'll go to my people,

And well will I speak unto them of the white men:
I will tell them that they are as leaves of the forest,
Very many and strong, and I'll not fight against them."

They left for New York, and upon their arrival
Near the wharf, they observed a large number of people,
Who had come to a place that was called "Castle Garden,"
To witness a man in a great bag, ascending
Far up in the sky, till no eye could perceive him.
'Twas a wonderful sight, and an Indian young man,
In awe-stricken tones enquired of the Prophet
If he had gone up to consult the Great Spirit.

Here the Indians received the most friendly attention:
At their rooms they were called on by both men and women,
And the great council house was thrown open one evening,
That they might be given a public reception.
They were shown everything it was thought would be
    pleasing:
The great public buildings, the halls of amusement,
The ships coming in o'er the wide, rolling ocean,
The theatre plays and the glittering fire-works.
They were feted and feasted and showered with presents.

On leaving New York, they went up the Hudson
By steamboat to Albany, capital city,
Thence westward to Buffalo, over Lake Erie,
And up to Detroit, where old friends were missing,
Around to Green Bay, then up the Fox River,
Across by the portage, and down the Wisconsin
To Prairie du Chien, and thence to Fort Armstrong.[160]

THE COUNCIL OF RELEASE

When the captives returned from their final release,
That henceforth they might follow the pathway of peace,
A call was sent out for the Indians to meet,
Both Saukies and Foxes, their brothers to greet.

In canoes they came up the great river and bore
The American flag to the Iowa shore.
Some time in completing arrangements was spent,
Then with songs and with shouts to the island they went,
Where they cordially greeted the home-coming band,
Extending to each one a welcoming hand.
After smoking the peace pipe they soon went away
To prepare for the council the following day.

In the morning the Indians, a hundred or more,
Came again to the fort from the Iowa shore:
Many white men were there, and the prisoner band
To be set free again, under Keokuk's hand.

Major Garland arose, and a reference made
To good feeling by all toward the Black Hawk displayed;
Then the words that the Washington Father had said
In his Baltimore specch he caused to be read,
And fully explained to the Indians there
By the well known interpreter, Antoine Le Claire.

Then the Chief, upon whom the Great Father relied,
Arose in his place, and with feeling replied:

"We have listened to the talk of our Great Father,
    Unto whom we pledged our honor for our friends:
We considered their condition in our councils,
    With such help as thought of wives and children
        lends.

"Families beseeching made us feel like women,
    But the while we knew that we were truly men;
And the words that we sent forward to our Father
    Worthy were of faithful Sacs and Foxes then.

"He has spoken as the Father of his children,
    Unto whom each one of them is very dear:
Big the Spirit made his noble heart in council,
    And our brothers by his action now are here.

"We receive them gladly once again in friendship,
    And our hearts to them indeed are very good:
Once they listened to the word of evil council,
    Now their purpose is to live as brothers should.

"Gladly will I give to them my hand in friendship,
    When they shake it they shake hands with everyone:
From the heart of Keokuk these words are spoken,
    When I grasp their hands again I shall be done."

The Chief of the Saukies concluded, and then
Major Garland addressed the assembly again.
He said that one thing should be well understood,
And he wished to make it just as plain as he could:
Keokuk, the Great Father acknowledged to be
Head Chief of the Sacs and the Foxes, and he
Would give counsel to which the Black Hawk should
    conform.
This raised in the breast of the old Chief a storm.
He sprang to his feet in resentment and pride,
Restraint thrown away, and in hot words replied:

"I am truly a man, and am wise, being old.
I will act for myself, and will not be controlled.
I gave counsel to many young men in my day,
Shall I be directed by other men?   Nay.
Very soon at the Great Spirit's call I shall go
Where I shall find rest.   While I tarry below,
I will give careful heed to our Father alway.
I have said it before.   I have no more to say."

Excitement was high, and the Head Chief, alone,
Seemed to know what to do.   At his side in low tone
He said to the Black Hawk, "Why do you speak so
Before the white men?   You trembled.   I know
That you did not mean all the things that you said.
I will speak to the council again in your stead."

The old warrior saw his mistake, and content
That his words be withdrawn, he nodded assent.
Then Keokuk spoke, very earnest and grave,
All concerned from a bad situation to save:

"Our brother has spoken, but not with his head
Or his heart, but with tongue that was forked instead.
He trembled as unworthy words he would say,
Like the oak tree whose roots have been wasted away.
Let the words of his tongue be as though they were not,—
He has said that he wishes they should be forgot.
He did not mean them, but his heart and his head
Speak in brotherly terms we'll remember instead.
I have spoken for him.   My words are his own.
Good words we should cherish, and good words alone.
So as we go forth, this thing let us say:
Our brother spoke well in the council to-day.' "

Then another good friend, the wise Davenport,
Colonel William, who then was in charge at the fort,[161]
Spoke words that were kindly and helpful that day,
And the spirit of evil was driven away.
Black Hawk was restored to his balance again,
And addressed the assembly of white and red men:

"I am an old man.   I am glad to be back
And meet with my brothers, the Fox and the Sac.
Full well do I know that their hearts have been good,
And they have done all that the best of friends could.
They have cared for my dear ones while I've been away,
And the Great Spirit knows that I thank them to-day.
Before the sunset on the morrow shall be
My wife and my children again I shall see.

"I told the Great Father that I would give heed
To Keokuk's counsel, and I will indeed.
It will not be my place any more to command.
But alone I shall live, without village or band.

"What I said in the council, let it be forgot.
Draw through it a line, or put on it a blot.
My speech was too quick, and I did not mean it.
Now we are alone, let us say, 'We forget.'

"Say to our Great Father and Governor Cass
That their counsel I'll heed as my few years shall pass.
Long before the war of last year was begun
I made my way toward the bright rising sun
To counsel with Governor Cass and to find
What things he might say to enlighten my mind.

"The counsel he gave I would not then receive,
Though that it was good I now fully believe;
But then I preferred that my counsel should be
Sent out by the Father across the great sea.
My father had listened to him in his day,
And I thought that I too should heed what he might say.

"Myself and my party, including each one,
Now thank our Great Father for what he has done.
We know that he means to do that which is best.
He and I are both old, and will soon be at rest.
By his order through many great towns we were sent,
And were treated with kindness wherever we went.

"We thank you, Major Garland, and Mr. Sprague too,
For being with us, and attending us through
The long, crooked way till at last we were here:
We knew we had friends when you two were near.
When you come to the great Mississippi again,
In my wigwam I hope I may welcome you men.

"I have no wigwam now, but I give you my hand.
As you go back you'll see where I lived with my band.
Though we meet not again, I'll remember you long.
The Great Spirit will give you and yours a good song.

To my own folks I'll go, ere shall rise the new sun.
I'll shake hands with my brothers, and then I am done."

Then Wapello rose to pronounce the last word,
For 'twas thought that the voice of a Fox should be heard:

"The habit of speech I have not. I will say
That I think, and that I have been thinking all day.
Keokuk has well spoken. With him I agree.
I am happy my brothers again here to see.
With joy I will take by the hand everyone.
I have spoken few words, and with them I am done."

When Wapello ceased, they shook hands all around,
And the best of good feeling was seen to abound.
The council adjourned. Ere the dawn of next day
Black Hawk to his dear ones was well on his way,
And in peace and in quiet he soon settled down
On the Iowa River near Keokuk's town.

White men crowded round Keokuk's Reservation,
And the Indians decided upon a removal.
Young Appanooce, Chief of a band of the Saukies,
Chose a site on the southerly side of the River
Des Moines, in what now is Wapello County.
"Ah-taum-way-e- nauk", was the name of his village,
The city or town of persistent endeavor:
The white men have shortened this name to "Ottumwa."
The Fox Chieftain, Wapello, settled below him.
A dozen miles farther and over the river,
Near the site of the fearful Sauk-Iowa battle,
Chief Keokuk's company made their new village.

Farther up the Des Moines were Hard Fish and his Saukies,
Where the fair town of Eddyville now is established.
Wapello's second band was on the Skunk River.
Poweshiek and his people removed farther westward,
Still keeping within the loved Iowa valley.
Other chiefs of less note were in charge of encampments.[163]

General Street, now the Agent for Saukies and Foxes,
Brought Catlin, the painter, to visit his charges.
This painter and writer was greatly delighted.
He described the Head Chief as of fine, portly figure,
With a very good countenance, open and friendly,
Clear and pleasing in speech and of dignified bearing.

He remained for a time and produced many portraits
Of chiefs and of warriors, of women and children.
The one that by all was most greatly admired
Showed Keokuk riding his favorite charger,
Said to be the best horse in the wide Western country.

THE SALE OF KEOKUK'S RESERVATION

In the year thirty-six, Keokuk's Reservation
Was bought by the Government, payment provided
By cash and annuities, sums paid to traders

IDA POWESHIEK, GREAT GRANDDAUGHTER OF CHIEF POWESHIEK,
AND PAPOOSE

To liquidate debts, and to widows and children,[164]
Amounted to nearly ten score thousand dollars.
Besides they were given two hundred good horses.

A request that was made for their early removal
Was met by the Indians present with laughter.
Apology followed and then explanation:
"We left long ago and have all sold our wigwams.
Chemokomen bought them for various prices,
As much as one hundred or two hundred dollars."

THE TREATY OF 1837

In the year 'thirty-seven the head Chiefs and warriors,
Some thirty in number, the choice of the nation,
Made a trip to the east with the Indian Agent
And Le Claire, the interpreter, portly and pleasant.
The Black Hawk by Keokuk's favor went also.

They were cordially greeted at Washington City
And, holding a council with Government agents,
Considered, discussed and concluded a treaty,
By which they made sale of a strip of their holdings
Lying west of the war cession, known as Scott's purchase,
And including full five quarter millions of acres.

For these fertile lands the U. S. made agreement
To erect near their villages agency buildings,
Break up and fence in for their use the raw prairie,
Maintain pattern farms and employ needed labor,
Put up shops and mills, hire blacksmiths and millers,
And make to the delegates suitable presents.

The Government also a new plan adopted
In dealing with Saukies and Foxes, agreeing
To put to their credit ten score thousand dollars
And pay to them yearly ten thousand in interest.
Some part of the income was subject to order,
Should the Indians wish, to promote education.

Eight months were allowed for the Indians' removal
From these purchased lands, though by special arrangement
The Sauks who resided at Keokuk's village
Were given two years to remain in possession.

A VISIT TO GREAT EASTERN CITIES

Their business concluded, the Agent conducted
The Indians to some of the great eastern cities.
Wherever they went they were heartily greeted,
And shown all the sights that were likely to please them.
Chief Keokuk ever was courteous to Black Hawk,
But the old warrior chose to remain in the back ground.

In New York, as it chanced, they attended a lecture
By Catlin upon "The American Indian,"
In which the great painter displayed many portraits.
When that of Chief Keokuk, riding his charger,
Was placed on the easel, the Indians shouted.

The great chief arose and apologized for them:
"I hope, my dear friends, you will pardon my people
For being excited and shouting so loudly.
The painting is perfect of both horse and rider.
Their surprise and delight has caused them to be noisy."

Someone in the audience made intimation
That no Indian ever possessed such a charger.
Le Claire, the interpreter, quickly responded,
That he had himself sold the horse to the Chieftain,
And that it was known as the best on the border.

In Boston a meeting was held at the State House,
And an eloquent welcoming speech was delivered
By the able and eminent Governor Everett.
Keokuk, "Cicero of his race," made the answer.
Other red men spoke also, including the Black Hawk.
Then a present was made to each one of the Indians:
Keokuk the great speaker and Black Hawk the warrior
Received each a sword and a fine brace of pistols.

THE LAST DAYS OF BLACK HAWK

In the year 'thirty-seven and eight in the winter,
Black Hawk and Asshawequa had an encampment
On a branch of the Devil's Creek, known as the Sugar,
In the westerly part of what now is Lee County.

One bitter cold evening there came to the wigwam
A. Cruickshank, well known in that part of the country,[165]
A burner of lime and a builder of chimneys,
Delayed on a trip to a settler's cabin.
He received a warm welcome, a supper and lodging.

Much refreshed by his sleep he awakened next morning
To find that his boots had been warmed with hot feathers,
And to sit down to breakfast, well fit for a monarch,
Of turkey and venison, white biscuits and honey.

The home was a picture of neatness and comfort,
An Indian dwelling of simple refinement;
But more than all else was the genuine kindness
So graciously shown by the host and the hostess
To the travel-worn white man delayed on his journey.

In the year 'thirty-eight, very early in spring-time,
The old warrior moved to a neatly built cabin
On the northerly bank of the fair Des Moines River,
Near the scene of the famous Sauk-Iowa battle.[166]
Here he quietly lived with his wife and his children.
The agent was careful to show him attention,
And other white men often called at his cabin.

By Fort Madison citizens he was invited
To join in a Fourth of July celebration
And speak as he chose to a toast at the banquet.
He gladly accepted and freely responded.
The toast and response are in paraphrase given:

"To our illustrious guest: May his declining years
Be as serene and free from warlike toils and fears
As has his former life been boisterous and rough.
He comes in friendship now, and we are glad enough
That he should have a place at this our festal board,
And share in all the good these modern times afford."

The Black Hawk replied: "I am with you to-day
Because the Great Spirit, who watches alway,
Has brought me to you.   I am glad to be here.
The white people now are to me very dear.

"I have eaten with you.   It is all very good.
Once I fought against you.   I then thought that I
        should.
Perhaps I did wrong.   Now the war sun has set,
Let us bury it all, let us say we forget.

"The Rock River land was to me very fair:
The village, the cornfields and all that was there.
I fought for it hard.   It is yours to-day
It will yield you good crops.   You should keep it
        alway.

"I thank the Great Spirit that now we are friends.
We stand side by side and we work for good ends.
I was once a great warrior, but now I am poor.
It is Keokuk who has brought ill to my door.[167]

"But I do not blame him.   I am old.   I have whiled
A long time.   This river I've loved since a child.
I was born near its banks.   I am near to life's ends.
I am glad to shake hands, and count you as my
        friends."

The Black Hawk returned to his riverside cabin,
Where he lived through the long, golden days of the summer.

The faithful Asshawequa saw he was failing,
And said: "He is old. Very soon he will leave us.
Sowana, the Great and Good Spirit, will call him."

A party of Iowas came on a visit
To the place that they once had accounted their homeland.
Ill feeling forgotten and all wrongs forgiven,
They held with the Black Hawk a council of friendship.
The spot where they met was north-west of his cabin,
And there the old warrior directed his body,
When death should o'er take him be decently buried.

When the gold and the crimson of autumn were coming,
The Indians went to the fort at Rock Island
To receive their annuities there from the Agent.
Black Hawk had expected to go, but was stricken
With fever, and therefore remained in his cabin.
For a few days he lingered and then he departed
To the hunting grounds fair where good Indians gather.

His body was buried as he had directed
With three days' provisions for him on his journey.
A mound was built up and a flagpole erected
From which waved the folds of the national banner.

Hardly nine months had passed when the tomb was invaded
By vandals and from it the body was taken.
Madam Black Hawk in grief called at once on her neighbor,
James Jordan, who started to search out the matter.
An appeal was soon made to Governor Lucas,
Who gave to the search all the help of his office.

The body had first been conveyed to Saint Louis,
The skeleton thence had been brought up to Quincy,
Where, having been wired, it waited in storage.
These things being known, the Governor promptly
Made out in due order and form requisition,
And soon the remains were brought up to his office.

Then he sent for Ne-som-see, a son of the Black Hawk,
And his brother, the handsome and brave Nah-se-us-kuk.
They came in great haste to the Governor's office,
And looked there upon the remains of their father.
"The place being dry", they considered it better
That there they should stay, and returned to their mother,
Who, bowed in her grief, was convinced and consented.

Shortly after, the Governor, thinking to give them
More fitting and permanent place, sent the relics
To the Burlington City Historical Building,
Where sixteen years later the fire consumed them.

O Black Hawk, fond lover of home and of homeland,
Of Saukenauk, long your own Indian village,
By the bright, flashing waters of Rock River rapids,
Of the graves in which slept your own fathers and children,
On the slopes of the hillside, the dear Chippiannock,—
And who long cherished hope to lie down there beside them!

Cast out from your village, you dwell in a cabin
By the still-flowing waters of River DesMoyen
And made second choice of a place to be buried,
Far apart and alone in a grave in the valley.

But fate was more kind than your uttermost wishes.
As your love for your land was as broad as the valley
Of the great Mississippi and all of its branches;
So your flesh cast aside and thrown out in Saint Louis,
And your bones turned to ashes and gas in the city
On the flint hills of Iowa, near the Great River,
Thus turned back to nature, are seen in the flowers,
The grasses and trees, the reeds and the rushes
And the beautiful birds that sing out in the branches;
And your spirit, it seems, in such incarnation
Is abroad evermore in the great fertile valley,

KEOKUK'S WIVES
From original photograph

From which your own race has departed forever,
Leaving it as the home of white men and their children.

THE DES MOINES RIVER AGENCY

Keokuk and his band by the Washington treaty
Had been granted the moons of two years for removal,
But on their return they were offered by white men
Some three thousand dollars to move in the spring-time.
They accepted the offer and made preparations
To transfer their wigwams and all their belongings
Twelve miles farther up and across the fair river,
Just below where Chief Wapello's band was established.

In March 'thirty-eight there came to the Agent,
From Commissioner Harris in Washington City,
Instructions to seek out a proper location
And begin the erection of Agency buildings.

The Agent, consulting the Indians, selected
A site to the north of the fair Des Moines River,
Near what is now known as Agency City.
A contract was let for erecting the buildings,
And others for breaking and fencing the prairie.
Saw mills and grist mills on each side of the river,
On Soap Creek below and on Sugar above it,
Were put up and equipped for the sawing and grinding.
Farmers and blacksmiths and millers and matrons
And all other helpers as needed were hired,
It being the purpose to make demonstration
Before all the Indians of white people's methods,
In hope that they, seeing how much was accomplished,
Would desire, themselves, to take part in the labor
And ascend to the heights of true civilization.

The efforts put forth for the Indians' advancement,
By the Government through its most excellent Agent,[168]
By selfish white men were quite largely defeated.

The traders sold freely to Indians on credit
And purchased in season their furs and their peltries.
When these became fewer, they took of the money
That was paid to their wards by the Government yearly.
As occasion arose they put down further charges
On the books to be paid when a Government purchase
Should provide further funds for the use of the red men.
The traders were counted as friends by the Indians
And exerted great influence always upon them,
But practically none toward their civilization.

Other white men there were, who were aptly called
   "wretches,"
Vile sensual fellows, debased and degraded,
Unlicensed as traders, but constantly selling,
Or trading to Indians for goods they had purchased,
That hell-broth of ages, the death dealing whiskey.

There was every appeal to the sensual nature
Of half savage people, compelled to stop fighting,
And because of the scarceness of game to be followed,
Denied in large measure the pleasures of hunting.
Although in their hearts the Indians despised them,
They bought the red liquor from these vile purveyors,
And like Noah of old they drank and were drunken.

With their native repugnance to manual labor,
Their freedom of purchase from Indian traders
And their fondness for liquor by bad men provided,
They could not or would not give any attention
To the art and the science of civilization.

Notwithstanding all this, they respected their Agent,
Good General Street, who had faithfully served them,
And when, in the springtime of 'forty, he left them
To take the long journey, they mourned his departure.

TAMPA INDIANS AT THE GRAVES OF GENERAL STREET AND WAPELLO
NEAR AGENCY CITY, IOWA

BLACK HAWK SPRING
In Crapo Park, Burlington, Iowa

The General's body was fittingly buried
Near the elm trees, not far from the agency buildings.
The body of Wapello, Chief of the Foxes,
By his own desire and that of his people,
Was later brought there and laid down beside it.
Major Beach, a West Pointer, was made the new Agent.
He was Street's son-in-law, and was very efficient.

A dif'rence developed among the red people
Regarding the method of annual payments
From Government funds by the Indian Agent,
The custom had been for the Chiefs to receive it,
Make payments to traders and give any balance,
As the records might show, to each Indian household.
Hard Fish was the leader of those who dissented,
And held that the payments should be made directly,
Leaving each man to settle accounts with the traders.

So sharp was contention without an agreement,
That annuities due in the autumn of 'forty
Were unpaid till July of the following summer,
And then, by a compromise, which was effected.
After that the new method in full was adopted
And payments were made on the family basis.

In the year 'forty-one the good Governor Chambers,
A man of high purpose and earnest endeavor,
Was appointed successor to Governor Lucas,
Who as first in that office had been most efficient.[169]

The in-coming settlers were crowding the Indians,
Their debts to the white men were constantly growing,
For labor they showed not the least inclination
And bad men were dragging them down to their ruin.

THE FIASCO OF 1841

The Government facing the sad situation
Had nothing to offer by way of solution,

Excepting to purchase more land from the Indians,
Remove them again and put forth further effort
To teach them the ways of true civilization.

The Indian Commissioner, T. Hartley Crawford,
From Washington came with a plan for the purchase,
And also with duly attested commissions
For himself, J. D. Doty and Governor Chambers
To act in a council with Saukies and Foxes,
And arrange the details of the purchase and payment.

All traders and other white men were excluded
That unhampered the Indians might reach their conclusion.
For the rest of their Iowa lands they were offered
Full payment of all of their debts to the traders,
And in cash or in credits a round million dollars,
Part of which should be used for a fine council building,
A house for each family, farms fenced and broken,
Good schools for their children and competent white men
As farmers and millers and blacksmiths to help them.

It seems no impression was made on the Indians,
They asked for more time to consider the matter,
(Perhaps they consulted with some white advisers,)
And at the last session refused to make treaty.

THE TREATY OF 1842

Not many moons after the Chiefs in the valley
Called upon Major Beach and expressed a desire
To sell to the Government part of their country.
Information was given to Governor Chambers,
Who now knowing well the influence wielded
On the Indian mind by the regular traders,
Appointed two men to go over their records,
And as far as they could make a proper adjustment
Of claims to be made on the Indian monies,
That might be received from the sale of their country.

In the year 'forty-two and the month of October
A council was held and all matters considered.
It continued some days, and outside of the sessions
The Indians freely consulted the traders.
The final result was an Indian treaty,
By which in due form the Saukies and Foxes
Conveyed to the Government all of the holdings
Remaining to them in the Iowa country.

The payments included the following items:
The discharge of their debt to the Indian traders,
In all to a full quarter million of dollars;
Eight tenths of a million to stand to their credit,
On which five per cent every year should be paid them:
To each principal Chief, so long as in office,
An annual stipend of half of a thousand;
To the widow of General Street, the good agent,
A section of land with the agency buildings;
(Though the Indians paid for the latter a thousand;)
And a home for themselves to the south-west in Kansas.
All offers of teachers and schools for their children,
Of houses and farms for themselves, and of training
In ways of the white man were promptly rejected.

By the terms of removal, each band was permitted
To stay in its village till late in the spring-time.
From then till two years from the following autumn,
They must keep to the west of a line north and southward
Through the banks of the White Breast, where rocks are
    red-painted;
After which they must go to the far lands in Kansas.

THE RACCOON RIVER AGENCY

In the meantime a site for new agency buildings
Was selected. It lay ninety miles up the valley,
Just east of the river, a mile and a quarter
Below where the "Coon" enters in from the westward,

And within what is now the Des Moines city limits.
There the various buildings were duly erected
And Raccoon River Agency sprang into being.

The Indians made their choice of locations,
And built up their villages, nearer and farther.
The traders, and dealers in "gew gaws" and whiskey
Found their places and carried on business as usual.
There was no pattern farm, and so wet was the season
That little was done in the way of production.

In the two years that followed the Indians wandered
About a good deal, did some hunting and fishing,
But more often were idle and frequently drunken.
The summers were fair, and some corn, beans and melons
Were raised, for the most part by toil of the women.

In the year 'forty-five and the month of September
Preparations were made for a final departure.
Keokuk, his old self, as to meet the occasion,
With promptness and firmness assisted the agent,[170]
His conduct recalling the Governor's statement:
"A remarkable man! How noble an Indian
He would be, but for his intemperate habits!"

With annuity money and plenty of horses
The Indians started away on their journey.
The Saukies were well on their way in September.
Some Foxes still lingered, but finally started,
And with few exceptions, before the eleventh
Of October, as set by the terms of the treaty,
They, too, had gone forth from the Iowa country
To find a new home on the wide plains of Kansas.

The Sauks and Foxes in Kansas
and Oklahoma

"Westward ho! for sunny Kansas!"
Thither went the Sacs and Foxes,
Not in answer to a summons
Or in search of new adventure,
But as yielding under pressure
And forsaking their own country.

Gains were greater than their losses:
Fair indeed was this new country;[171]
There were rivers gently flowing,
Wooded bottoms, beauteous prairies,
Sights and sounds to cheer and please them.
Larger were the yearly payments,
Quite sufficient to provide them
With the things that most they needed;
Bad white men were still among them,
But in greatly lessened numbers;
And the Government endeavored
To protect them and to lead them
In the ways of better living.

In the year of eight and forty,
When the buds of spring were swelling,
From his home beside the river
Of the swans' own gentle mother,[172]
Keokuk, the great peace chieftain,
Passed beyond the veil of shadows
To the land of peace eternal.

Near the Agency, his body
In a well marked grave was buried.
Thence in 'eighty-three 'twas taken
To the beautiful bluff city,
That had been named in his honor.

On the highest elevation
Kindly hands again interred it,
And a monument upbuilded.

Moses Keokuk, or "Junior,"[173]
Like his sire in form and feature,
Like him too in mind and spirit,
Took his place, and long continued
Head Chief of the Sacs and Foxes.

Very careful were the agents,
Very wise and very careful,
And some bands were more responsive
Than had been the case aforetime.
By the good year eighteen fifty,
More than half a thousand acres
Were in truly Indian cornfields.
Two years later in a schoolhouse,
That of logs had just been builded,
Stood a son of T. H. Benton
Teaching eager Indian children.

Missionaries came among them[174]
With the old time Gospel message,
And were not without a welcome.
Drinking bouts were far less frequent,
And there came to be a number
Who were known as strict abstainers.

Keokuk, the son, was reckoned
As progressively progressive.
His own cornfields and his dwelling
Were examples to the tribesmen.
He believed in education,
Was attentive to religion,
And in time became a preacher.[175]

KEOKUK JUNIOR OR MOSES KEOKUK
From original photograph

MR. AND MRS. JOHN EARL KEOKUK

Mr. Keokuk is a Great Grandson of Chief Keokuk

Pot-a-quaw and good Che-kus-kuk
Both were chiefs, who lived in houses
And accorded with the Head Man.
Mo-ko-ho-ko represented
Those resisting all advancement.

In the year of six and sixty
William Irwin, Special Agent,
Made report to the Department:
That the shops were well conducted,
And in school the Indian children
In deportment and advancement
Seemed to equal those in white schools;
That the Agent, Major Martin,
Had been uniform in treatment
Of all classes of the Indians,
And that under him improvement
Had been made in their condition;
That the Chiefs who were progressive
Had cooperated with him;
And that all the opposition
Came from those preferring wild life.

The "Diminished Reservation"
Of the Sauk and Fox in Kansas
Was disposed of by a treaty
Made the fall of eight and sixty.
By its terms one year thereafter
All the Indians were to leave it
For a home in Oklahoma.

When the time approached for leaving
Many protests and objections
Were brought forward by the Indians,
And a council of officials
And of chiefs and braves was summoned.

It was held upon a greensward
With fine shade trees all about it.
Round the group of those in council
In a circle were the Indians,
And beyond, an outer circle
Of the whites was closely gathered.

The Commissioners presented
All the facts about the treaty,
And the benefits to follow
Both to red men and to white men.
Keokuk and Mo-ko-ho-ko
Each delivered an oration,
Both objecting to removal,
But in closing, one consenting
And the other one refusing.

Soon thereafter all the Indians
Were removed to Oklahoma
And placed on a reservation
In what now is Lincoln County.

Mo-ko-ho-ko and his Indians
Soon returned, and years thereafter
Spent more time in sunny Kansas
Than they did in Oklahoma,
But were finally ejected
By the military forces
In the fall of six and eighty.

.   .   .   .   .   .

Oklahoma, home of Indians!
Thither went the Sacs and Foxes
In the fall of nine and sixty,
Nevermore to be pushed farther.

Many years have passed, and slowly,
With the Government to guide them,

KE-KE-BE-NO (BILLY JONES)
Tama Indian, overseas soldier in the 88th Division, in dancing pose

MRS. JONES
Weaving

They have followed paths of progress.
Old wild ways have been abandoned,
Farms and homes and schools and churches
Have been counted of more value,
And to-day they stand beside us,
Citizens of this Republic.[176]

The Meskwakis of Tama County Iowa[177]

The Foxes who lived on the Iowa River,
Apart from the bands of their brothers and cousins
Near the Agency on the fair River DesMoyen,
Were even more loath to remove from their country
To the home selected for them out in Kansas.

They went under protest, but never were happy
Near the Agency, where there were efforts to bring them
Along the broad pathway of civilization.
Some few, saving up their annuity money,
Returned to their haunts on the Iowa River
And bought land for themselves, as though they were white
        men:
Others rapidly followed, and more land was purchased,
It all being held as a common possession.
The Indians were peaceable, only desiring
To live their own lives in their own native manner;
White neighbors were kindly and well disposed toward them;
The State Legislature passed laws of permission;
And the Governor served as trustee for their holdings.

They lived for the most part in primitive wigwams,
Did hunting and fishing, made bead work and baskets,
Raised patches of corn and of beans and of melons,
And received some assistance from generous neighbors.

The Government urged them to go back to Kansas,
In the meantime withholding their annual payments.
But though they were wretched and poor they insisted:
"We live on our own land, and no reservation."

18

At length they prevailed, and the Government yielded:
An Agent was sent and annuities paid them.
Through the years that have passed they have been con-
    sidered
The ultra-conservative band among Indians.

In more recent times they have made great advancement:
The most of them now are living in houses,
They are raising good crops and have schools and churches,
And persuaded at last, are a civilized people.

JAMES POWESHIEK, GRANDSON OF CHIEF POWESHIEK, AND FAMILY   *f*

XXI. INCIDENTS AND TRIBUTES

RED BIRD'S CONTRIBUTION TO CIVILIZATION[178]

WHO brought to his death the world-famous Cock
    Robin?
Who gave Billy Patterson that awful wallop?
Who planted the trees in Tesson's apple orchard?
The Sparrow made boast of the Cock Robin murder.
The Patterson case has not yet been decided.
Red Bird has the call as the apple tree planter.

These apple trees stood tall and strong in the forest
Near the site of Montrose by the broad Mississippi,
And yielded their fruit, as do others, in season.
Who planted them there? Was it Red Bird, the half-breed?

Ere the Frenchman, Tisson, had come into that region,
Red Birds wick-e-up was beside the great river.
Every year he went down to the post at Saint Louis.
A friend at Saint Charles on such an occasion,
A che-mo-ko-man, gave him, wrapped up in a bundle,
Petite apple trees, in number some twenty,
And told him how best to plant out and protect them.
He carefully carried them back to his wigwam
And planted them out here and there in the forest.

This story is told by a settler named Kilbourne,
Who had it from Red Bird, himself, and moreover
Says that Black Hawk and other old Indians confirmed it.

Note this as additional proof of the story:
Red Bird was a half-breed, and in him were blended
The instincts of both the white man and the Indian.
No Indian in those days would plant out an orchard,
No white man would plant apple trees in a forest,
A half-breed might do both, *Quid Est Demonstrandum.*

Till at last,—O heart of woman!
O-pe-tos-ke-la, the faithful,
Seemingly by better effort
Than was put forth by his rival,
Touched her wrist, and was her husband.

Back they came from o'er the prairie,
Husband, wife and vanquished lover,
And the throng of friends and kinfolks,
Talking, laughing, racing, shouting
To conclude the Saukie wedding.

TRIBUTE TO BLACK HAWK[187]

O mighty War Chief of the great Saukie Tribe,
O patriot warrior, what pen can describe
The character elements that are combined
In your Indian heart and your Indian mind!

A love of your country as strong as your life,
And an equal devotion to children and wife,
With a hatred of foes, both of white men and red,
And a boastful delight in the blood you have shed;

A frank recognition that Indian bands
May make right of might and take each other's lands,
But a protest most strong that no white men should be
Accorded such rights on this side the great sea;

A keen satisfaction with Indian life,
And no wish for advancement by hard toil and strife;
A noble contempt for white men's evil ways,
But for their great virtues few tributes of praise.

With a will as imperious as Cæsar's could be,
You rejected all counsel that did not agree
With your purpose and plan, while flattering men
Deceived and misled you again and again.

BLACK HAWK STATUE
In Spencer Square, Rock Island, Illinois

Your Rubicon crossed, you refused to turn back
Till you knew that the soldiers were hot on your track;
Then you raised the white flag. With no reason therefor
It was scorned, and nothing could follow but war.

It was waged to the knife in true Indian style,
Your squaws and your little ones hidden the while,
And many there were who before you went down,
Yielding up to your braves the prized part of the crown.

What the white man alone was unable to do,
By famine's assistance was wrought against you:
You showed a real greatness in skillful retreat,
But were caught at the last in most crushing defeat.

A true Indian always, you stood for the right
As you saw it, and for it were willing to fight;
So that even when vanquished you held up your head,
And where blame might have come received praises instead.

In the square at Rock Island, your own native town,
Whose fame is enhanced by your greater renown,
Your image in granite looks forth with clear gaze,
From a place in the sward near the crossing of ways,
And you seem to speak out to each man passing by:
"Lo, you are one man and another am I."

But a monument that is more fitting for you
Is the noble Watch Tower, with wonderful view,
By nature prepared to bear onward your name
Through the long years to come, and to keep bright your
        fame,
As the Chief, so by love of his village obsessed,
That he fought against fate, nor would be dispossessed
Till the last blow was struck, and himself and his band
Were completely o'erwhelmed and removed from the land.

And the musical voice of each sweet-singing bird,
That in groves on The Tower in spring may be heard,
Shall speak of Asshawequa, joy of your life,
Your own Singing Bird and your one, faithful wife.

TRIBUTE TO KEOKUK

O Chief of the far-off vision,
   O Chief of the steady nerve,
Who could boldly meet every issue
   And never falter nor swerve!

O warrior, patriot, statesman,
   O orator, matchless in power,[188]
So gifted with insight and foresight
   As to be the man of the hour!

O Saukie Chief, true to your nation
   And true to the white man as well,
Who held back your people from slaughter
   And taught them in concord to dwell!

You belong not alone to the red race,
   O warrior-apostle of peace,
The great heart of humanity holds you:
   Your renown among men shall not cease.

On the bluff in the beautiful city,
   That honors itself with your name,
Your mortal remains are now sleeping
   'Neath a monument speaking your fame;

While above, a bronze statue heroic,
   Your image, as standing in life,
Looks out o'er the broad Mississippi,
   No longer the pathway of strife;

And we feel that though gone you are with us,
   A part of the peace of to-day,
And a Prophet of that great to-morrow
   When peace everywhere shall have sway.

KEOKUK MONUMENT
In Rand Park, Keokuk, Iowa

Dr. A. M. Stocking
(Samp-we-te-oh)

NOTES TO ILLUSTRATIONS

a. The statue was dedicated Saturday afternoon, July 1st, 1911. Seven hundred citizens of Oregon and vicinity attended, and a special train with two hundred people came from Chicago. Mr. Frank O. Lowden presided. The program included an original poem, "The Pine Forest," by Elia W. Peattie, an address by Edgar A. Bancroft, and responses by two speakers of Indian blood, Miss Laura M. Cornelius representing the Oneidas, and Dr. Charles Eastman, the Sioux. Hamlin Garland read a poem on "The Trail Makers," and Lorado Taft, after a vigorous demand from the audience, gave a short explanation of how the idea of the statue was conceived and put into execution. As is well known, this is the Black Hawk Country, and the statue is usually called by that warrior's name. But it was, in fact, not intended to represent any one Indian, but simply "The Indian," to typify the race.—*Richard V. Carpenter* in Journal of the Illinois State Historical Society for January, 1912.

The figure stands on land owned by Wallace Heckman, whose summer home, as also that of Mr. Taft, is near by. Says Mr. Taft:

"This is the way it happened. Every evening as the shadows turned blue, we walked over this bluff. We always stopped to rest at this point. As we stood here we involuntarily folded our arms in an attitude restful, reverent, and it came over me that generations before had done so. And so the figure grew out of the attitude, as we stood and looked on these beautiful scenes.

"I did not study any one type or race of Indians. It is a composite of the Foxes and the Sacs, the Sioux and the Mohawks, and, in short, it represents the Indian Personality. I have left off the usual Indian trappings, the feather and buckskin and other conventional signs. There is even a hint of the old Roman in the face, which was necessary to make it suggest a spirit unconquered while still the conquered race. To be suggestive rather than direct is what I aim at,—to do that is the great joy of the sculptor."

The statue stands on the east side of Rock River, about three miles above Oregon, Illinois. The bluff at that point is two hundred fifty feet high. There is a strongly built base, rising six feet above the surface. The figure itself is of concrete, forty-two feet in height and weighing two hundred sixty-eight tons.

The photograph from which the illustration has been made was sent the writer by Mr. Taft, and is the one which he considers the best. Following is a copy of a later letter received from him:

My Dear Dr. Stocking:

I appreciate your kindness in writing me and in sending the thrilling lines which you have written on my statue.

With best wishes,

Cordially yours,

LORADO TAFT.

b. From the Hauberg Collection, Rock Island, Illinois.

c. From the Anschutz Studio, Keokuk, Iowa.

d. From "The Black Hawk War" by Frank E. Stevens.

e. Furnished by Ben H. Wilson, Mt. Pleasant, Iowa.

f. Obtained through Joseph Svancina, Tama, Iowa.

g. Furnished by Mrs. John Earl Keokuk, Portland, Oregon.

h. Portraits of Black Hawk, Wapello and Shabbona from "The Black Hawk War" by Frank E. Stevens, that of Keokuk from the Anschuts Studio, Keokuk, Iowa. The portrait of Black Hawk was originally taken from the painting by R. M. Sully in the rooms of the Wisconsin Historical Society at Madison, that of Wapello from "McKenney and Hall's Indians." The pictures of Keokuk and Shabbona are from photographs.

i. The picture of the rebuilt Block House from the Hauberg Collection, that of the restored Davenport House furnished by Col. D. M. King, Commandant of the Rock Island Arsenal.

j. Portraits of George Davenport, Antoine LeClaire and John W. Spencer are from the Hauberg Collection, that of John Dixon from "The Black Hawk War" by Frank E. Stevens.

k. Portraits of John Reynolds, Henry Dodge and William Clark are from "The Black Hawk War" by Frank E. Stevens, that of John Chambers from "John Chambers" by John Carl Parish, with the permission of the State Historical Society of Iowa.

l. Portraits of Andrew Jackson, William Henry Harrison and Abraham Lincoln are from "The Black Hawk War" by Frank E. Stevens, that of Zachary Taylor from the Hauberg Collection.

m. The picture of Mary Kakaque is from the Hauberg Collection, that of Dorotha Keokuk from a kodak negative taken on the campus of the Indian School at Chilocco, Oklahoma.

NOTES TO TEXT

1. Paraphrased from an incident narrated in "History of the Island of St. Domingo from its First Discovery by Columbus to the Present Time," published in London in 1818.

2. Hayti, Hispianola or St. Domingo was the first of the large islands to be exploited by the Spaniards. The gentle and indolent natives were enslaved and compelled to toil in the mines and on the plantations. Those who resisted or escaped from servitude once entered upon, were pursued to their mountain fastnesses and hunted with dogs and guns as rebellious slaves. Their numbers were greatly depleted, others were brought in from adjacent islands, and when their extermination was foreseen, Negroes were imported from Africa to take their places.

3. Champlain founded Quebec July 3rd, 1608. The expedition against the Iroquois was undertaken about a year later. It was on this expedition that Lake Champlain was discovered and named.

4. The arquebuse (är-kwē-bŭs) was a large musket with a swinging support that was used as a rest when the gun was fired.

5. Opitchipan and Opechancanough were younger brothers of Powhatan. Opitchipan was the elder, and hence was recognized as the Emperor after Powhatan's decease. But Opechancanough was more ambitious and energetic and became the real ruler.

6. A few weeks after this treaty was made, Edward Winslow and Stephen Hopkins were sent to Massasoit's home at Sowams on a visit of compliment. They were to present to him a fine red coat, to suggest payment for corn taken by the colonists from caches on their arrival at Cape Cod, and to arrange for further trade. They were entertained in Massasoit's own wigwam, sleeping on the foot of the bed occupied by himself and wife. The writer of this book is a descendant of Stephen Hopkins.

7. *James D. Rishell* in notes to the edition of "Black Hawk's Autobiography" edited by him.

8. "Black Hawk's Autobiography."

9. Saginaw, originally "Sauk-e-nong" or place of the Sauks.

10. By the treaty of Paris, at the close of what is known in this country as the French and Indian War, Canada and its dependencies, including the posts along the lakes and the Ohio were ceded to Great Britain. This was resented by the Indians who formed a conspiracy under Pontiac, the great Ottawa Chief, to reestablish the French or

19

take posssession themselves. Plans were laid to secure admission to twelve fortresses at the same time, on various pretexts. Within two weeks of the time set, nine had been taken. The intrigue was not successful at Detroit, where Pontiac was in personal command, and after a siege of nearly a year he was compelled to withdraw. The various tribes included in the conspiracy soon sued for peace. The Sauks were probably living at Green Bay at this time, and had come to Mackinac to do their part in carrying out the plot.

It was the writer's privilege in 1924 to see a game of baggatiway, or la crosse, played by the Onondaga Indians at their Reservation south of Syracuse, New York.

11. Various travellers have stated that these villages were more substantially built, that more land about them was tilled, and that in other ways there was more evidence of a trend towards civilization among the Sacs and Foxes than among other northwestern tribes.

"The name Prairie du Chien is derived from that of an Indian Chief of the Fox tribe whose village was on the prairie. His name in the Indian language means Dog, a popular name among Indians, which in French is Chien. Prairie du Chien, therefore, does not mean prairie dog, as some persons have believed, but Prairie of Dog, or Dog's Prairie."—*William S. Hoffman in "The Campion," the students' magazine of Campion College, Prairie du Chien, Wisconsin.*

12. It is not easy to determine just what tribes held lands in succession through the years. These statements, however, seem to be correct. The Santeaux, who were a branch of the Chippewas, sometimes called Chippeways or Ojibways, are generally believed to have been the early occupants. French maps published about 1680 indicate that the Kickapoos were then in possession, and Black Hawk states in his Autobiography that the Sauks and Foxes drove the Kaskaskias out when they came.

13. Other villages were scattered here and there along the rivers. One occupied by the Foxes, and later presided over by Wapello, is said to have been at what is now Spencer Square, Rock Island, Wapello's wigwam being on the site of the New Harper House. Black Hawk speaks of Wapello as Keokuk's adopted brother.

14. Colonel Davenport told J. W. Spencer that as nearly as he could ascertain the Saukies had been in occupancy of the country about sixty years when the Black Hawk war broke out.

15. The Portage des Sioux lies between the Mississippi and the Missouri rivers about fifteen miles above their confluence.

16. Among the Indians of the upper Mississippi the Sacs and Foxes are decidedly the best actors and have the greatest variety of plays

among them. Their war dances may be viewed as tragedies in the rudest state; and those dances wherein both sexes appear are truly comedies of no mean cast. Each person who acts is painted and dressed in a manner entirely appropriate to the character to be presented. To see a play acted of a ludicrous character, I have seen a thousand Indians present who were delighted with the acting. Thunders of applause followed some antic prank, while a visible displeasure would sometimes punish a failure to act well.—*Atwater.*

17. The Frenchman fell from the main cliff, just in front of where the hotel and observation house now stands. It is sometimes called "The Frenchman's Cliff."

18. The place of this tragedy was the big spring grotto, once known as "The Cave of Death," and later as "The Maiden's Bower." Since the fall of the rock it has been known as "The Lover's Tomb." Black Hawk states that the event occurred in 1827.

19. The universal rule among Indians is that a brave is one who is known to have killed one or more enemies, while he who may have participated in a dozen or more pitched battles is but a warrior until it is known that he has killed and scalped an enemy. "The Sauks and the Black Hawk War."—*Armstrong.*

20. This incident is said to have occurred in a Pottawatomie band. The Pottawatomies were friends of the Sauks, and some of them gave aid in the Black Hawk War.

21. Both were great men in every sense of the term,—orators, warriors, patriots and statesmen.—*Armstrong.*

22. Black Hawk's own account of his life is followed very closely. The matter regarding Keokuk is drawn from various sources.

23. Black Hawk gives the tradition that Nanamakee or Thunder, under the direction of the Great Spirit, met the son of the King of France in Canada, who told him that he should supersede his father and become the head of the tribe. The old Chief readily acquiesced and called a council of all the nation at which Nanamakee explained the matter. Some were unwilling to accept his authority. As discussion went on a violent thunderstorm arose, and the lightning struck and set fire to a tree near by. Nanamakee, "being a very shrewd young man," told them that he had caused the storm, and that it was an exemplification of the name the Great Spirit had given him. All were then satisfied.

24. "The Black Hawk War."—*Stevens.*

25. According to Armstrong Black Hawk must have been made a sort of brave by brevet, his full right to that title to be confirmed when he should have slain an enemy.

26. It was not an uncommon thing for Indian warriors to desert under disappointment or discouragement, and it was generally considered to be more of a reflection upon the leader than upon the deserters themselves. Black Hawk tells us of his own withdrawal from the British forces in Canada, as follows: "I was now tired of being with them, our success being bad, and having no plunder. That night I took about twenty of my braves and left for home."

27. The Merrimac is a small river which enters the Mississippi a little way below St. Louis.

28. They say that a long while ago their fathers had a lodge, in the center of which were ranged four fires. By the first stood two Chiefs, one on the right hand who was called the Great Bear, and one on the left hand who was called the Little Bear. These were the Peace or Village Chiefs. They were the rulers of the band, and held the authority that we would describe as that of Chief Magistrate, but not in equal degree, for the Great Bear was Chief and the other next in authority. At the second fire stood two Chiefs, one on the right hand called the Great Fox, and one on the left called Little Fox. These were the War Chiefs or Generals. At the third fire stood two braves who were called, respectively, the Wolf and the Owl; and at the fourth stood two others who were the Eagle and the Tortoise. The last four were not chiefs, but braves of high reputation, who occupied honorable places in the council, and were persons of influence in peace or war.

The lodge of four fires may have existed in fact, or the tradition may be merely metaphorical. The Chiefs actually rank in the order presented in this legend.—*Armstrong.*

29. This conflict was known in America as "The French and Indian War," but in Europe it was called "The Seven Years War." In 1849 Governor Dinwiddie of Virginia, under orders from England, had granted to the Ohio Company a half-million acres of land on the Ohio river, between the Alleghany and the Kanawha. Settlement was resisted by the French, who erected a fort at the junction of the Alleghany and the Monongahela. Washington was sent with a letter of expostulation, and later as second in command of a force to engage the French soldiers. By the death of his superior officer, Colonel Fry, he was left to direct the battle, which resulted in the defeat and death of Jumonville.

30. The English and French did not scruple to use
Red men against white and the act to excuse
On the ground that in war any thing may obtain
That will help your own forces a victory to gain.

31. This treaty was made at Paris Feb. 10th, 1763. The lands beyond the Mississippi had been secretly ceded by France to Spain the year before.

32. This proclamation was made Oct. 7th, 1863, and declared it to be "Our royal will and pleasure—to reserve under our royal protection and dominion, for the use of Indians, all the lands and territories lying to the westward of the sources of the rivers which fall into the sea from the west and northwest—and we do hereby strictly forbid, on pain of our displeasure, all our loving subjects from making any settlements whatever or taking possession of the lands above reserved, without our special leave and license."—*Wisconsin Historical Collections*, XI, pp. 46-52.

33. For a condensed statement of these grievances see the Declaration of Independence.

34. General Henry Hamilton was Lieutenant Governor of Quebec under Governor Sir Guy Carleton. He was in charge of the western regions that had been included in that province under the act of 1774, and had his headquarters at Detroit. He excused himself for directing the Indian atrocities on the ground that he was acting under orders. The rewards of the Indians were called presents, but they were always in proportion to the visible evidences of accomplishment.

In September, 1777, Hamilton reported directly to Lord George Germain, Secretary of State for the Colonies in the King's Cabinet, as follows: "At the best computation which can be made eleven hundred and fifty warriors are now dispersed over the frontiers. Seven hundred are on the list who have had their equipment, or at least amunition from this place." Early in 1778 he wrote General Carleton that the Indians had "brought in seventy-three prisoners alive, twenty of which they presented to me, and one hundred and twenty-nine scalps." In September of the same year he wrote to General Haldimand, who had succeeded General Carleton as Governor, that "since last May the Indians in this district have taken thirty-four prisoners, seventeen of which they delivered up, and eighty-one scalps."

Many soldiers in the Black Hawk War were descendants of settlers in Kentucky and Ohio who had been killed by Indians. Abraham Lincoln was one of these.

35. Colonel Clark did not meet Lieutenant Governor Hamilton directly until the second taking of Vincennes by the Americans.

36. Patrick Henry was then Governor of Virginia.

37. Prairie du Rocher and Saint Philips, villages lying between Kaskaskia and Cahokia were also taken by Clark's forces.

38. Colonel Clark's spelling of these names is here used.

39. This place had never been out of his mind, and in conference with Gibault, who was the chief priest of all the French towns, he learned that Abbott, the English Governor, had left Vincennes shortly before, and that the fort and town were at that time virtually in the possession and control of the French inhabitants. "Conquest of the Northwest."—*William H. English.*

40. Lieutenant Governor Hamilton left Detroit October 7th, 1778, and reached Vincennes on December 17th.

41. This news was brought by Francis Vigo on January 29th, 1779. Clark marched with his forces on February 5th, the fort was assaulted on the 23rd and surrendered the next day.

42. Much credit belongs to Clark's men, but most belongs to their leader. The boldness of his plan and the resolute skill with which he followed it out, his perseverance through the intense hardships of the midwinter march, the address with which he kept the French and Indians neutral, and the masterful way in which he controlled his own troops, together with the ability and courage he displayed in the actual attack, combined to make his feat the most memorable of all the deeds done west of the Alleghanies in the Revolutionary War. It was likewise the most important in its results, for, had he been defeated, we would not only have lost the Illinois, but in all probability Kentucky also. "The Winning of the West."—*Theodore Roosevelt.*

43. This was the Northwest Territory, which included what is now the states of Ohio, Indiana, Illinois, Michigan, Wisconsin and a part of Minnesota. At the peace conference in Paris in 1782, Great Britain desired to hold this territory as a part of Quebec, but the fact that it had been largely conquered by Clark and was still held by the Americans greatly weakened her claim. France, though not unfriendly to the new nation, wished to have this territory turned over to her ally, Spain. The American Commissioners, John Adams, John Jay and Benjamin Franklin were handicapped by a resolution of Congress, which provided that they were to undertake nothing in the negotiations for peace without the knowledge and concurrence of the Ministers of the King of France. Under the leadership of the far-sighted Jay this resolution was disregarded and the preliminaries of a separate treaty with Great Britain were entered into, by which the United States was confirmed in the possession of this territory and Britain agreed to abandon the forts she still held there. The completed treaty, which was signed September 3rd, 1783, confirmed this action.

"The principal merit of the negotiations was Mr. Jay's."—*John Adams.*

"It was not only chiefly but solely through his [Mr. Jay's] means that the negotiations of that period were brought to a successful conclusion."—*Lord St. Helens.*

44. Spain's declaration of war against Great Britain was made in May, 1779.

45. This force consisted of about a thousand men, mostly Indians. Chief Wabasha led the Sioux contingent. Matchekuis, a noted Chippewa Chief, is said to have commanded the other Indian allies.

46. *James D. Rishell.*

47. Colonel John Montgomery, who had been left in command at Kaskaskia by General George Rogers Clark, is said to have commanded the Spanish and American forces, which consisted of about three hundred fifty men. "Long Knives" was a name originally given by the Indians to the Kentuckians, but it came to be applied to all Americans.

48. This battle was fought on a branch of the Wabash, which was at first supposed to be a tributary of the Maumee.

49. This treaty was made at Fort Greenville in 1795.

50. On the completion of the negotiations, Robert Livingston, who had been the leading representative of the United States government, said to all present: "Gentlemen, we have lived long, but this is the noblest work of our whole lives. This will change vast solitudes into flourishing districts."

Napoleon Bonaparte said: "A few lines of a treaty restored to me the Province of Louisiana, and repaired the fault of the French negotiator who abandoned it in 1763. But scarcely have I recovered it when I must lose it. But this I promise you: It shall cost dearer to those who oblige me to strip myself of it than to those to whom I deliver it; for I have given England by this act a rival on the high seas, that will one day humble her pride."

51. Our policy will be to form New Orleans and the country on both sides of it on the Gulf of Mexico into a state; and as to all above that, to transplant our Indians into it, constituting them a *Mare Clausee,* to prevent emigrants crossing the river, until we have filled up all the vacant country on this side.—*President Jefferson to M. Du Pont De Nemours.*

52. The heading of the treaty is as follows:

"Articles of a Treaty, made at St. Louis in the District of Louisiana, between William Henry Harrison, Governor of Indiana Territory and the District of Louisiana, Superintendent of Indiana Affairs for the said Territory and District, and Commissioner Plenipotentiary of the United States for concluding any treaty or treaties, which may be found necessary with any of the Northwestern tribes of Indians, of the first part; and the Chiefs and Head men of the United Sac and Fox Tribes on the other."

The Instrument was signed by William Henry Harrison, and by Pashepaho or the Stabber, Head Chief of the Sauks, Quashquamme or Jumping Fish, Outchequaha or Sun Fish, Hashequarequa or The Bear, and Layowvois or Laiyuva. Eleven interpreters, secretaries, military men and citizens signed as witnesses.

53. This man was a relative, perhaps a brother of Quashquamme, one of the Chiefs who signed the treaty. There are various accounts of the murder for which he was apprehended. There appears to be no record, other than the statements of the Indians, concerning his release and assassination.

54. This is the entry for the first day: "Sailed from my encampment on Friday, the 9th August, 1805; with one sergeant, two corporals and seventeen privates, in a keel boat 70 feet long, provisioned for four months: water very rapid: encamped on the east side of the river at the head of an island."

55. The special object of the expedition was to explore the headwaters of the Mississippi, and to deal with the more northerly tribes and traders. Hence the part of the river on which the Saukies resided was passed over very rapidly, both in going and coming back. Pike returned to St. Louis April 30th, 1806.

56. These rapids are in the Mississippi, their lower end being a few miles above the mouth of the Des Moines. They have ceased to be as such because of the building of a great dam at Keokuk.

57. Whiskey that is three-fourths water.

58. "Puants" or "Stinkers" was a name given to the Winnebagoes by the French.

59. "Sateurs" or "Salteurs" was a name given by the French to a band of Chippewas, not because they were fine jumpers, but because they lived by the tumbling waters of the Sault St. Marie. It has been variously corrupted and widely used to designate all Chippewas.

60. Ewing Agricultural Station.

61. The British traders.

62. "As to the matter of planting the American flag at the Watch Tower Village, I know of no other material on the subject than that mentioned by you. [Pike's Journal and Black Hawk's Autobiography.] If Pike did what Black Hawk says he did as to the flag, Pike evidently

forgot to write it in his diary, and Black Hawk on the other hand fails to mention Pike's return trip, when everybody was 'spoiling for a fight' at Black Hawk's village."—*John H. Hauberg.*

63. At this time Lieutenant Alpha Kingsley. The company landed at the site and proceeded to the erection of the fort in September 1808.

64. Lieutenant Thomas Hamilton was in command on this occasion, as also later when the fort was evacuated.

65. Elsk-wa-ta-wa, the Prophet, was a brother of the great Tecumseh and associated with him in his opposition to the aggressions of the whites. Tecumseh was at this time in the South seeking allies among the Indians there.

66. This declension was no doubt influenced by Black Hawk's inordinate vanity and aversion to play second fiddle to any man. He never brooked the idea of a Superior Officer and boasted that he had won an hundred battles and was never defeated. Had the "Couchant Tiger" offered to make him Commander in Chief of the confederacy, he and his band would doubtless have joined it.—*Armstrong.*

67. This was the famous battle of Tippecanoe. It was fought before Tecumseh's return from the South and, as he thought, prematurely. He blamed his brother severely for having entered into it.

68. The statements here made regarding the action of the trader and the Captain are given on the authority of Black Hawk. The writer has been able to find no confirmation or denial from other sources. That a message from Washington might have failed to reach them is not difficult to understand; but it is well-nigh beyond comprehension that any trader should have known so little about the customs of the day in dealing with the Indians, or that the officer of a post, at such a critical time, would not have insisted upon his complying with their reasonable request for credit.

69. Dixon had long been a British trader among the Indians and was well known by them. It was doubtless for this reason that he was commissioned as a Colonel and sent out to enlist as many of them as possible under the British standard.

70. The Fort Dearborn massacre occurred August 15th, 1812. The Pottawatomie Indians under Chief Senachwine had surrounded the fort, and the garrison had agreed to surrender it to them on condition of being allowed to proceed to Ft. Wayne without molestation. To this the Indians consented, but when they discovered that the powder and liquor had been destroyed, they set upon the departing whites and massacred most of them.

71. Fort Meigs, so named in honor of Governor Meigs of Ohio, was on the Maumee river, where on May 1st, 1813, General Proctor with a force of about five thousand British and Indians besieged General William Henry Harrison.—*Rishell.*

72. The soldiers who came down the river in boats were General Green Clay's Kentuckians. One detachment of these pursued the British too far and were defeated and captured, as Black Hawk says, but the other detachment was instrumental in raising the siege.—*Rishell.*

73. The interference of Tecumseh and Black Hawk, when the Indians were killing the prisoners, is well known in history. Tecumseh was under peculiar obligations to protect the white prisoners, having given General Harrison his promise that this should be done. At one time during the siege, the prisoners were undergoing rough treatment at the hands of the Indians, while General Proctor was standing helplessly by. Tecumseh, riding up at the moment, leaped from his horse in great anger, and threatened to kill the first one who laid a hand upon the prisoners. "Why did you permit this"? he angrily demanded of General Proctor. "I am unable to restrain your warriors," was the reply. "You are unfit to command," cried Tecumseh. "Go home and put on petticoats."—*Rishell.*

Notwithstanding the efforts of Tecumseh and Black Hawk, many American prisoners were massacred by the Indians in this war. Their practice of denying the right of sepulture to slain foemen was also enforced. General Proctor and the other commanders seemed to consider that the Indians, fighting for their homes and lands, had a right to make use of their own methods of warfare. So far from terrorizing the Americans, however, it stimulated enlistments and aroused them to greater valor.

74. This fort was located at Lower Sandusky. The attack was made on August 1st, 1813 by five hundred British regulars and seven hundred Indians. The garrison consisted of about one hundred fifty Americans, under command of a young lieutenant, George Croghan, a nephew of George Rogers Clark.

75. Other defeats for the British followed. Perry's famous victory on Lake Erie was won on Sept. 10th, 1813, Detroit and Malden were soon evacuated, and on Oct. 5th Proctor was defeated by Harrison at the battle of the Thames and Tecumseh was slain.

76. His departure was strictly in accordance with Indian notions of military discipline. "No success and no plunder" justified a desertion at any time. A Chief was obeyed, not because of his office and rank, but because of his ability to lead his people to successful war.—*Rishell.*

77. This man was Elijah Kilbourne, who met Black Hawk again at the time of Stillman's defeat.

78. The French town of Peoria was burned early in November of 1812 by a force of Illinois militia sent out by Governor Edwards under command of Col. Thomas E. Craig. It had been charged that the inhabitants had distributed arms furnished by British traders to the Indians, and otherwise encouraged them to act against the Americans. It was also claimed that the boats of the soldiers were fired upon at night by the inhabitants or by their Indian friends.

The upper Indian Village, near the head of Peoria Lake, was later destroyed by a force under Gov. Edwards himself, John Reynolds, who was Governor at the time of the Black Hawk War, being a member of the party.

79. This battle was fought July 19th, 1814. Sixteen white people were killed, including one woman and one child. Black Hawk says that he lost only two of his warriors. These were killed by the fire from Rigg's boat. The state of Illinois has erected a monument to commemorate the event.

Lieutenant Rigg's name is more frequently spelled with a final "s."

80. William Clark was a brother of George Rogers Clark, and was co-leader with Meriweather Lewis of the great north west exploring expedition of 1803-6. He was appointed Governor of Missouri Territory in 1813 and served as such until its admission as a state in 1821. The following year he was made Superintendent of Indian Affairs, which position he held until his death in 1838. The new fort at Prairie du Chien was named Fort Shelby in honor of the Governor of Kentucky. Later it was called Fort Crawford, in honor of the Secretary of war.

81. Zachary Taylor, (Old Rough and Ready,) the great hero of the Mexican war and President of the United States, did not fill a very heroic role in this engagement; but doubtless the wisdom and discretion that he showed in retiring promptly from an impossible situation was a factor in his later success. This battle was fought Sept. 5th, 1814.

82. Indian scouts had reported the coming of Taylor's boats to Black Hawk, and in the night the guns had been moved farther down and suitably mounted.

The large island to which the Indians retired, called Credit Island or Suburban Island, lies near the Iowa shore opposite the mouth of Rock River.

83. This fort was called Fort Edwards in honor of Ninian Edwards, Governor of Illinois Territory from 1809 till its admission as a state

in 1818, and again Governor from 1826 to 1830. He was also a United State Senator and one of the most eminent men of his day. The site of the fort in the city of Warsaw is marked by a suitable monument.

84. The British Commissioners—stated as a preliminary, without which all further discussion would be useless: that the Indians must be included in the pacification, and a permanent boundary established for them, beyond which the United States should never purchase, settle or occupy any territory. This region, which should be included between the Indian boundary and the British possessions, was to remain forever uninhabited except by Indians, and be a permanent barrier between the British and American territories. The boundary proposed, subject, however, to some modifications, was the same as that of Wayne's treaty at Greenville in the year 1795, and would now include within the Indian lines a territory as extensive as one-quarter of the United States, and one hundred thousand white inhabitants. "A History of the Political and Military Events of the Late War between the United States and Great Britain." (Published in 1825.)— *Samuel Perkins.*

Lord Gambier, Henry Goulburn and William Adams were the British Commissioners. John Quincy Adams, James A. Bayard, Albert Gallatin, Henry Clay and Jonathan Russell represented the United States. The treaty was signed at Ghent, Belgium on Dec. 24th, 1814 and was ratified Feb. 15th, 1815.

85. Artile IX of the treaty is as follows: "The United States of America engage to put an end, immediately after the ratification of the present treaty, to hostilities with all tribes or nations of Indians with whom they may be at war at the time of such ratification, and forthwith to restore to such tribes or nations, respectively, all the possessions, rights or privileges, which they may have enjoyed or been entitled to in one thousand eight hundred and eleven, previous to such hostilities. Provided, always, that such tribes or nations shall agree to desist from all hostilities against the United States of America, their citizens and subjects, upon the ratification of the present treaty being notified to such tribes or nations, and shall so desist accordingly. And his Britannic Majesty engages on his part to put an end immediately upon the ratification of the present treaty, to hostilities with all the tribes or nations of Indians with whom he may be at war at the time of such ratification, and forthwith to restore to such tribes or nations, respectively, all the possessions, rights and privileges which they may have enjoyed or been entitled to in one thousand eight hundred and eleven, previous to such hostilities. Pro-

vided, always, that such tribes or nations shall agree to desist from all hostilities against his Britannic Majesty, and his subjects, upon the ratification of the present treaty being notified to such tribes or nations, and shall so desist accordingly."

86. Every day affords a new proof that the Rock River Sacks intend to continue the war. They have been notified of the pacification by the military commander of this district, as well as by Governors Clarke and Edwards; yet they still continue their war parties on the frontiers of St. Charles County, and murder all those who are so unfortunate as to come within their reach.—*Niles Register,* May 20th, 1815.

Some palliation for these outrages may be found in the fact that the British on the northwest frontier, long after they were officially notified of the peace, continued to incite the Indians to acts of violence against the United States, and, indeed, participated in them likewise. "Life of Black Hawk."—*Benjamin Drake.*

87. Fort Howard was near the mouth of the Couvre River, which enters the Mississippi on the Missouri side a short distance above the mouth of the Illinois.

Black Hawk states that this raid was conducted shortly after his return from the British front, to revenge the wanton killing of his adopted son by the whites; but the historical records fix the date as May 24th, 1815. This was a year and three quarters after his return and just five months after the signing of the treaty of peace. Another statement from his Autobiography serves to explain the discrepancy:

"My memory, however, is not very good since my late visit to the white people. I have still a buzzing noise in my ears from the noise and bustle incident to travel. I may give some parts of my story out of place, but I will make my best endeavors to be correct."

88. The loss to the whites was eight killed, five wounded and one missing. They found the bodies of seven Saukies on the battlefield or nearby, and a bloody trail led to where the canoes had been.

89. The treaty with the Missouri band of the Sauks was made on September 13th, 1815, and that with the Foxes on the following day. Both were signed by William Clarke, Ninian Edwards and Auguste Chateau, Commissioners Plenipotentiary of the United States, and were duly witnessed. Twelve Sauk Chiefs and warriors, including Quashquamme, signed the Sauk treaty, and twenty-two Fox Chiefs and warriors signed the Fox treaty.

Treaties with twelve Indian tribes were made within a few days.

90. On August 30th, 1813, the Creek Indians attacked Fort Mims,

near the junction of the Alabama and Tombigbee rivers, in what is now the state of Alabama. They suffered severe losses, but finally captured the fort and massacred more than four hundred of those who were gathered there. General Jackson organized an army, and by forced marches reached the Indian country and in three battles, fought on November 3rd and November 9th, 1813 and March 27th, 1814, killed over a thousand Creeks, with comparatively small loss to his own troops. Some knowledge of these events had reached the Indians as well as the whites.

91. The Foxes returned. They said, "We have smoked the pipe of peace with our enemies, and expect that the Americans will send a war party against you if you do not go down." This I did not believe, as the Americans had always lost by their armies that were sent against us. La Gutrie and other British traders arrived at our village in the fall. La Gutrie told that we must go down and make peace, as this was the wish of our English father. "Autobiography."—*Black Hawk.*

92. This treaty was signed on May 13th, 1816, by William Clarke, Ninian Edwards and Auguste Chateau on behalf of the United States, and by twenty-two Sauk Chiefs and warriors, including Black Hawk.

93. Colonel George Davenport was the first citizen of Rock Island in point of time, and up to his death undoubtedly the first in standing and influence. His home on the island, built in 1831, is still standing and is one of the most interesting historical structures in the Mississippi Valley.

94. Antoine LeClaire was the son of a French Canadian trader. His mother was the daughter of a Pottawatomie Chief. Both parents were members of the Catholic Church, according to the rites of which they had been married. Mr. LeClaire was educated in St. Louis, and received his appointment as interpreter through General William Clarke, Commissioner of Indian Affairs. He was a man of fine character, thoroughly reliable and efficient, and became the founder of the cities of Davenport and LeClaire.

95. Colonel William McKay had been in command of the British forces that captured Fort Shelby at Prairie du Chien on July 17th, 1814.

96. "History of Illinois."—*Davidson and Stuvè. Iowa Historical Record,* Vol. VII, pp. 190, 191.

97. Governor Ninian Edwards was a dignified and polished gentleman, and in his time the best known and most influential man in Illinois. He had been Chief Justice of the Supreme Court of Kentucky, Governor of Illinois through the entire period of its separate

existence as a territory, and U. S. Senator for six years previous to his election as the third Governor of the state. Shadrach Bond was the first state Governor, and Edward Coles the second.

98. Governor Edwards, who placed no confidence in Indian promises or Indian friendship, was not idle in his attempts to rid the state of the different Indian tribes still within its borders. Having got rid of the Winnebagoes, he continued with much persistency to urge upon the war department the pressing necessity for removing all the Indians beyond the state. He saw very clearly from the events of the last few years, that the red and white men could not live together in the same vicinity without committing reprisals upon each other and promoting hostile feeling. His first communication was written as early as the 4th of September, 1827, in the course of which he said that, "The occupancy by the different tribes, of the ceded lands, and their constantly traversing every part of them at their pleasure, without any right to do so, could no longer be submitted to." He particularly mentioned the Pottawatomies, who resided near Peoria, on lands which had not only been ceded, but actually granted by the Government to individuals. He regarded it as "A grievance inconsistent with the rights of the state," and the respect of the President for those rights ought not to permit him to hesitate to do his duty in the premises." "History of Illinois from 1778 to 1833 and Life of Ninian Edwards."—*Ninian W. Edwards.*

99. Governor Reynolds was known as "The Old Ranger," from the fact that he had served as a ranger in the war of 1812. Personally he was quite the opposite of Governor Edwards, but he was a shrewd politician and a man of energy and ability.

100. Keokuk was now recognized as the head Chief of the Sauks.

101. Winneshiek, the Prophet, was the son of a Sauk Chief and a Winnebago squaw. In accordance with Indian usage he was considered a member of his mother's tribe. His village was on Rock River at the site of Prophetstown. His claims as a Prophet were recognized by Sauks as well as Winnebagoes, and he was frequently consulted by them.

102. This was the spring of 1829.

103. Judge John W. Spencer was one of the first settlers of Rock Island, and throughout his long life one of its best known and most highly respected citizens.

104. This was April of 1830.

105. This was the spring of 1831.

106. Major General Edmund P. Gaines commanded the Western Department of the army, with Headquarters at Jefferson Barracks

123. General Atkinson had brought with him from Jefferson Barracks six companies of the Sixth Infantry, totaling two hundred twenty men. He obtained two companies from Fort Crawford, under command of Lieutenant Colonel Zachary Taylor.

124. The army was organized with Samuel Whiteside as Brigadier General. There were four regiments. John Thomas was Colonel of the First, Jacob Fry of the Second, Abraham B. DeWitt of the Third and Samuel M. Thompson of the Fourth. Majors James D. Henry and Thomas James commanded spy battalions, and Major Thomas Long a foot battalion. Abraham Lincoln was Captain of a company in the Fourth Regiment. Two other battalions under Majors Isaiah Stillman and David Bailey had been called to meet the army at Dixon's Ferry.

125. At the time of the Black Hawk war all the north part of the state was an unbroken wilderness, except a few trading posts and the mining settlement about Galena. The country was in possession of Indians, had not been surveyed by the Goverment nor been explored to any great extent by the hunter or pioneer.

In 1827, a road was opened direct from Peoria to Galena, connecting the mining region with the settled part of the state, and known as Kellogg's Trail. . . . A few persons located on this road for the purpose of entertaining travelers and keeping stage teams.

With the exception of the Peoria and Galena road, all thoroughfares in the unsettled parts were only trails, and traveled alike by whites and Indians. . . . The largest settlement north of the Illinois River was on Bureau Creek, consisting of about thirty families. A few cabins were built north of the great bend in the Illinois River, and on the site of Peru; two at LaSalle, eight or ten on Indian Creek, five or six at Holderman's Grove, and a number about Plainfield. A few families had settled on Fox River as high up as Newark, and there was quite a settlement in the vicinity of Ottawa. "Memories of Shaubena" (1878).—*N. Matson.*

Dixon's Ferry was on Kellogg's Trail. It was owned and operated by John Dixon, who lived there with his family and also kept a store and tavern. Mr. Dixon was a man of fine character, and was held in the highest esteem by white men and Indians alike. Black Hawk and his band camped one night near the ferry on their way up the river, and Black Hawk, Winneshiek and Nahpope ate at Dixon's table.

126. The Territory of Michigan at that time included what is now the state of Wisconsin. There were some settlements at Milwaukee and Green Bay, but more in the lead mines region above Galena.

Henry Dodge was Colonel of Militia for this part of the Territory, and one of the most efficient leaders in the war.

127.   Dixon's Ferry, May 12th, 1832.
To Major Isaiah Stillman:

You will cause the troops under your immediate command, and the battalion under Major Bailey to proceed without delay, with four days' provisions, to the head of "Old Man's Creek," where it is supposed there are some hostile Indians, and coerce them into submission.

John Reynolds,
Com. in Chief of the Illinois Militia.

128. The names of the slain men were Captain John G. Adams and privates David Kreeps, Zadok Mendinhall and Isaac Perkins, all of Tazewell County; Sergeant John Waters, Corporal Bird W. Ellis and privates Tynes M. Childs and Joseph B. Farris of Fulton County; and Gideon Munson, a scout.

129. Governor Reynolds excuses this disaffection in the following statement: "They said the truth, that they had volunteered in such a hurry to protect the frontiers, and had arranged to remain in the service only a short time, as they expected the Indians would be chastized in a few days. They had no clothes with them, and many of their families were not provided for at home. These were all true statements, I knew; and I knew, also, that the term of their enlistment was undefined and they had power to return after the service they had done.

130. Nearly forty years after the death of Shabonee, the Shabonee Memorial Association of Grundy County was formed and in the latter part of October in about the year 1900, a monument to the memory of Chief Shabonee was erected in Morris, Illinois, at the head of his grave. It is a huge boulder of gray granite, weighing many tons, and across a smooth side of it is inscribed, "Shabbona, 1775-1859."—*Alta P. Walters in Journal of the Illinois State Historical Society, October,* 1924.

131. The next year after this tragedy occurred, James Hayes made a claim here and built a cabin by the side of a spring, where the residence of William Knox now stands. Around the tree where Sample and his wife were burned, Mr. Hayes noticed many human bones and in a ravine near by a skull was found. But little was thought of this affair at the time, as these bones were supposed to be those of Indians. . . . Some of the early settlers had noticed this tree, and still recollect its being burned at the root. . . . This place with its surroundings has undergone a great change. To the

east in plain view lies the city of Princeton with is beautiful land-scape scenery. . . . The old burr oak tree, where the victims suffered and around which the Indians danced, has long since fallen by the woodman's ax, but its stump still remains as a relic of the past. "Memories of Shaubena." (1878).—*N. Matson.*

132. Kee-was-see was a Pottawatomie Indian, who had been caught and severely beaten by Davis, when he was attempting to break up the dam so that the fish could ascend the stream.

133. The brains of children were dashed out against a stump; the women were butchered, and, after the most revolting mutilations, were hanged, heads downward, to neighboring trees.—*Stevens.*

The scene of the massacre is about fourteen miles north of Ottawa. A monument, bearing the names of the murdered ones was erected on the spot by William Munson, and is still standing. In 1906 a park, known as Shabbona Park, was laid out there and a more sub-stantial monument built, an appropriation for the purpose having been made by the state.

134. The amount of ramsom is not clearly known. It seems to have been paid largely in ponics and trinkets.

The following year Sylvia Hall was married to William S. Horn and Rachel Hall to William Munson. A granddaughter of Mrs. Munson became the wife of the Hon. James H. Eckles, Comptroller of the Currency under President Cleveland.

135. Jacob Fry was made Colonel of this regiment. The Captains were Samuel Smith, Benjamin James, Elijah Iles, George McFadden, William C. Rolls and Adam Snyder. Many who had been officers reinlisted in the ranks. Captain Lincoln became a private in Iles' company, and Brigadier General Whiteside himself served in the same capacity under Snyder.

136. Burr Oak Grove was a part of Kellogg's Grove.

137. As a matter of fact there were seventeen in the party of Indians; eleven were found dead, two were killed in crossing the river or swampy widening of it, and were scalped by the Winne-bagoes; Colonel Hamilton, when he came up, found the body of another; and late the succeeding winter a French trapper found three more in the swamp close by, beneath brushwood, under which they had crawled when wounded.. "Bourchard's Narrative."

138. Jacob M. Early was Captain of an independent scouting com-pany, that reported directly to General Atkinson. Abraham Lincoln re-enlisted for the second time as a private in this company.

139. Isaac Funk had settled at Funk's Grove near Bloomington. He was a man of fine character, widely known and respected.

140. There were some Winnebagoes with Colonel Dodge; and Colonel William S. Hamilton, a son of Alexander Hamilton, and a man of affairs in the region of the lead mines, commanded a small forces of Sioux and Menominees.

141. On the 10th of July, in the midst of a considerable wilderness, the provisions were exhausted, and the army forced to abandon the pursuit of the enemy for a short time. Seeing the difficulties to reach the enemy, and knowing the uncertainty of ever finding Black Hawk by these slow movements, caused most of the army to believe we would never overtake the enemy. This condition of affairs forced on all reflecting men much mortification and regret, that this campaign also would do nothing. Under these circumstances a great many worthy and respectable individuals, who were not particularly operative in the service, returned to their homes. My staff and myself left the army at the Burnt Village on Rock River, above Lake Koshkonong, and returned by Galena to the Frontier and home.—*Governor Reynolds.*

142. The Wisconsin River.

143. These canoes were made by taking sections of bark from the large elm trees on the bottom, shaving the ends and tying them together as only Indians could do. Before daylight of the 22nd nearly a hundred women and children and old men had embarked on these frail craft. They were intercepted by a small party of regulars sent out from Prairie du Chien by General Street, the Winnebago Indian Agent. Fifteen men were killed, and thirty-two women and children and four men were taken prisoners. Many more were drowned, while others, who escaped to the woods, with very few exceptions, perished with hunger or were massacred by a party of Menominees from Green Bay under Colonel Stambaugh.—*Wisconsin Historical Collections.*

144. Reports differ as to the losses sustained in this battle, though all white authorities agree that the militia had one man killed and eight wounded. Dodge says there must have been forty Indians slain. Reynolds and Ford put the number at sixty-eight with many wounded. Stevens says that sixty-eight Indians were killed, and the bodies of twenty-five, who had been wounded, were subsequently found on the trail to the Bad Axe. Black Hawk reports six Indians killed, but says nothing of the wounded. He concludes that the losses of the whites must have been greater in proportion, as their force was large, while but fifty of his men engaged in the battle.

145. Black Hawk says: "I would not have fought there but to gain time for my women and children to cross to an island. A

warrior will duly appreciate the embarrassment I labored under, and whatever may be the sentiments of the white people in relation to this battle, my nation, though fallen, will award to me the reputation of a great brave in conducting it."

His claim has been fully conceded by white men, who unite in saying that his manner of conducting the battle so as to hold the army in check showed great generalship.

146. Early in the morning of the 22nd Henry dispatched an express to General Atkinson in forming him of the battle, and Colonel Dodge sent a letter to General Street, asking him to intercept those coming down the Wisconsin in Canoes.

James D. Henry and Henry Dodge were the most able and efficient officers in the Black Hawk War. Henry had been a Lieutenant in the War of 1812, and was well fitted to command. It was his courage and resolution in transcending the orders of General Atkinson that led to the discovery of Black Hawk's line of retreat, which he followed in vigorous pursuit. He was in command at the battle of Wisconsin Heights, and though later Atkinson sought to keep him in the back ground, he won chief honors at the battle of the Bad Axe. Stevens says of him in "The Black Hawk War": "His inflexible regard for duty, even in the face of criticism and intrigue, moved him forward with the irresistible force of a glacier and. . . pushed him forward to be the most popular man in the state of Illinois, and very soon the nominee of his party for Governor. Had he lived nothing could have prevented his election. He died of pulmonary consumption at New Orleans, March 4th, 1834, at his hotel lodgings.

Colonel Dodge was spared to a great career as Governor, Senator and leading citizen of Wisconsin.

147. Black Hawk says that even before they left their encampment to journey towards the Mississippi they had been in great straits for food, being forced to dig roots and bark trees to obtain something to satisfy hunger and keep themselves alive. Many did actually die from starvation.

148. Black Hawk in his autobiography does not claim to have had any part in the battle of the Bad Axe, but other writers concede his presence and the leadership of the band that drew Atkinson away.

149. It was only a comparative safety, for some of them became the victims of their hereditary enemies, the Sioux.

150. Seventeen white men were reported killed, and twelve wounded. The slain of the Indians was estimated at about one hundred fifty, while it was thought that as many more were drowned.

About forty prisoners were taken, mostly women and children. Others, including Black Hawk and his two sons and Nahpope and the Prophet, were brought in later by the Winnebagoes.

151. This was Lieutenant Robert Anderson of Fort Sumpter fame. He was an artillery officer of the regular army at that time, and served throughout the Black Hawk war as Assistant Inspector General.

152. There is some uncertainty as to where this incident occurred. In the Kansas Historical Collections, Vol. XI, P. 355, it is stated that it was the Wisconsin River near its mouth that was crossed at a time "during the Black Hawk war when the Sauks and Foxes were hard pressed." The squaw was Mrs. Julia Mitchell. She went to Iowa with the other Indians, and on July 4th, 1840 at the Des Moines River Agency she was married to John Goodell, a white man, who was one of the interpreters, a member of the Methodist church and wielded a wide influence for good. At the Agency in Kansas the Goodells were quite prominent, and Mrs. Goodell has been referred to as the most remarkable woman of her tribe.

The little papoose, Mary Mitchell, was adopted by Lieutenant William Hill at Fort Crawford. The Lieutenant soon died and the child was taken by a settler at Prairie du Chien, named Moore. She was educated at a Quaker school in Philadelphia, and married Thomas Means, a white man who deserted her. She then went to live with her mother and step-father at the agency, where she married an Indian.

"I had an interview with the lady who was the child at the time. She was nintey-three years of age when I saw her in 1918, at her home at the Sac and Fox Agency, not far from Prague, Oklahoma. She was the widow of Moses Keokuk, who was a Baptist Minister, son of Chief Keokuk."—*John H. Hauberg.*

153. Major General Winfield Scott was another great man who had a part in the war. He ranks with the best of those in the nation's history, who have combined high character and great abilities.

154. The Missouri Republican of September 11th, 1832 contains a statement that the steamboat, Winnebago, arrived in St. Louis, en route for Jefferson Barracks, ten miles below, on September 10th, that the boat left Galena with Black Hawk, The Prophet, two sons of Black Hawk and nine braves, together with about fifty warriors. The latter were landed south of the lower rapids on their pledge of neutrality. Black Hawk, The Prophet, two sons and nine braves were taken to Jefferson Barracks to remain as hostages. On the preceding Thursday, Nahpope and six or seven warriors were taken

there by Lieutenant Cross and five men under his command. —*Stevens*.

155. Black Hawk states that he was treated very kindly by The White Beaver, except that he was placed in irons upon his arrival, which humiliated him very much.

156. This treaty was made and signed September 21st, 1832. Fearing recurrence of cholera on the island, the council was held on the Iowa side at a point near what is now 420 West Fifth St. in Davenport. Mr. LeClaire built a house on the site in 1833, which is still standing.

Four hundred square miles of land on the Iowa River, including the site of Keokuk's village, were reserved for the Indians; and at their special request one section, now within the city limits of Davenport, and one section at the head of the rapids, where the village of Le-Claire is located, were reserved and granted to Antoine LeClaire, the Interpreter, whose mother was a Pottawatomie and whose wife was a Sauk.

157. Colonel Davenport, Interpreter LeClaire and other old friends of Black Hawk were in this party.

158. The prisoners were Black Hawk and his two sons, Nasine-wiskuk and Nahseuskuk, Winneshiek, Nahpope and perhaps some others. Keokuk and his wife and little son, Pashepaho and Appanooce, Sauks, and Wapello and Poweshiek, Foxes, were invited guests. The Interpreter, LeClaire, Colonel George Davenport, S. S. Phelps and William Courland also went along. When the prisoners were sent to Fortress Monroe, the others returned to the west, with the exception of LeClaire, whose presence as Interpreter was necessary.

159. The prisoners were taken to Fortress Monroe on April 26th, and released from there under charge of Major Garland on June 4th. President Jackson met them at Baltimore and addressed them on June 6th.

160. They arrived at Fort Armstrong about August 1st.

161. Colonel William Davenport was a U. S. army officer, who had served in the Black Hawk War. He was not related to Colonel George Davenport. Marmaduke S. Davenport, who began his duties as Indian Agent at Rock Island on January 1st, 1833, was not related to either of the others.

162. Later this strip came to be known at The Black Hawk Purchase.

163. These removals were not all made at the same time, but the various bands finally came to be located as indicated.

164. A noteworthy item was a thousand dollars to be paid to the

widow of Felix St. Vrain, the Sac and Fox Agent murdered early in the Black Hawk war.

165. This story was told to the writer by J. P. Cruickshank, a son of Alexander Cruickshank, and one of the leading citizens of Fort Madison.

166. There has been some dispute regarding the place of Black Hawk's residence in the Des Moines valley, some contending that it was on the south side of the river. He may have lived on that side at one time, but it seems to have been pretty well established that his residence at the time of his death was on the north side. Following is an extract from a letter written by James H. Jordan under date of July 15th, 1881 to Dr. J. F. Snyder of Virginia, Illinois:

"Black Hawk was buried on the Northeast Quarter of Section 2, Township 70, Range 12, Davis County, Iowa, near the Northeastern corner of the county, on the Des Moines River bottom, about ninety rods from where he lived at the time he died, and on the north side of the river. I have the ground where he lived for a dooryard, it being between my house and the river."

The location is on the site of old Iowaville between Selma and Eldon.

167. Towards Keokuk he entertained feelings of bitter antagonism, which were never reciprocated, so far at least as external indications went, by Keokuk. The hate seemed to exist upon the part of the old Chief only.—*Armstrong.*

168. General Joseph M. Street was one of the best and ablest men, who had to do with Indian affairs in Illinois, Wisconsin and Iowa. He was a Kentuckian by birth, and coming to Illinois was appointed General of Militia by Governor Edwards. As Government Agent for the Winnebagoes he did valuable service in the time of the Black Hawk war, and later as Agent for the Sacs and Foxes at Rock Island and the Des Moines River Agency he was most faithful and efficient.

Among the traders were George Davenport and Russell Farnham, Antoine LeClaire; S. S. and William Phelps; Francis Labachiere; Pratte, Chouteau & Co.; G. W. and W. G. Ewing; and J. P. Eddy. Some of these represented The American Fur Company, organized by John Jacob Astor, while others were independent.

Mr. W. Oscar Couchman of Carthage, Illinois, an uncle by marriage of the writer, was a babe in arms at the Des Moines River Agency, his father, Judge W. O. Couchman, being at that time an employe of S. S. Phelps & Co. Keokuk's wife frequently called upon the young mother, and took great delight in helping to care for the little white pappoose.

169. Both Governor Lucas and Governor Chambers were excellent men, having the good of the Indians at heart. Governor Lucas was appointed in 1838 by the VanBuren administration, but according to partizan usages, had to give place when the Harrison-Tyler administration came into power.

John Chambers was an eminent Kentucky lawyer. He served as Aid-de-camp to General Harrison in the war of 1812, and later was a Member of the Kentucky Legislature and a Representative in Congress. When General Harrison became President, Mr. Chambers acted as his private secretary, and on March 25th, 1841 was appointed Governor of the Territory of Iowa and Superintendent of Indian Affairs in that region. He continued in office till November, 1845, when James Clark of Burlington, Iowa was appointed by President Polk to succeed him. See "John Chambers" by John Carl Parish, published by the State Historical Society of Iowa.

170. It is a pleasure to transact business with him, because of his aptness to understand motives and arguments, and to appreciate the condition of his people, while his readiness to co-operate and to forward every measure suggested by me, merits the approbation of the department.—*John Beach.*

171. The Sauk and Fox Agency in Kansas embraced, generally speaking, all of Weller (now Osage) County south of Dragoon Township, to the present Coffey County line, and extended six and one-half miles east into Franklin County, and some three miles west into Lyon County.

172. The Marie de Cynges River.

173. The Indian name of the son of Keokuk and his wife No-kaw-qua-le, who succeeded his father as Chief was Waw-naw-ke-saw, but it was very seldom used after his father's death. He was known as Keokuk Junior, and very soon simply as Keokuk. The name Moses was given to him in later years. He was born at Saukenauk in 1824, and died in Oklahoma in 1903.

174. The Rev. Richard P. Duvall was the first Missionary to the Sac and Fox Indians in Kansas. He was appointed by the Kansas Methodist Conference in 1860, and with the exception of the year 1862-63, when he was chaplain of the Sixth Kansas Volunteers, continued until 1866. His wife, Sarah, acted as school teacher. During their stay great impetus was given to education and religion. Charlie Keokuk, son of Chief Moses Keokuk, spent one summer vacation with Mrs. Duvall at her old home in Delaware, Ohio, much to his

delight and benefit. Joe, the son of Chick-a-skuk, the leading Fox Chief was also greatly benefited by the schools.

175. There were many influences that brought about Keokuk's conversion. His growing appreciation of the white man's path as trodden by the better class of pale faces, his own success as a farmer and a man of affairs, his interest in education and the general welfare of his tribe, and his admiration for the character and work of the Duvalls were among them.

He attended a sacred concert given by Philip Philips and his band of singers at Baldwin, Kansas, where his son was in school, and was much impressed, saying, "Surely there must be something in the white man's religion after all. He sought counsel of Mr. and Mrs. Goodell and of William Hurr, an Ottawa Indian Interpreter, who was also a Christian. On Mr. Hurr's suggestion, and with him as a companion, he attended a series of meetings held by a Baptist Missionary named Isaac McCoy, where he professed conversion and joined the Baptist Church. He was ordained as a Minister in 1876 in Oklahoma, built a church at his own expense and preached in it a part of the time. Mrs. Fanny Goodell Nadeau said, "It was inspiring to see and hear Keokuk preach. He made a beautiful prayer."

After the death of his first wife Moses Keokuk married Mrs. Mary Means, the daughter of Lieutenant David D. Mitchell and his Indian wife, Julia, later Mrs. John Goodell. See note 152. Mrs. Mary Keokuk lived very happily with her illustrious husband and testifies that he lived a truly Christian life for at least thirty years before his death.

176. Black Hawk was survived by two sons, Nah-se-us-kuk and Nas-in-e-wis-kuk or Ne-som-see, the spelling of these names being variously given) and one daughter, Nam-e-qua. There are numerous worthy descendants in later generations. The family name in the direct line is "Ka-ka-que."

Keokuk's son and successor, No-kaw-qua, better known as Keokuk Junior or Moses Keokuk, died in 1903, leaving one son, Charles Keokuk who passed away the following year. He was survived by three sons: Frank R., John Earl and Robert, and one daughter, Fanny, all of whom are well educated and worthy citizens. It was the writer's privilege to meet with Miss Dorotha Keokuk, a daughter of John Earl Keokuk, in the Indian school at Chilocco, Oklahoma in the spring of 1924.

This school is one of the best in the country. The interest taken and the progress made by the students is remarkable. The writer attended a preliminary contest in music, which was excellent, and also witnessed two debates of Indian students with representatives of the high school at Arkansas City, Kansas, in which the Indians won.

Among the more prominent Sauk Indians of later years may be mentioned Prof. William Jones, noted ethnologist and philologist; Dr. Thomas Miles, Physician and Surgeon; and Walter Battice, for many years Secretary of the tribe.

When asked some time ago regarding any grievances the Indian race might have against the whites, Mr. Battice wrote as follows:

"As to grievances, we as educated Indians have come to the conclusion that it is too late to serve any good purpose by going into the matter of right and wrong, concerning the early and recent relations between the aborigines of this country and the other races, the invaders of the Indian domain, etc. What we wish to do is to equip ourselves for what is coming, cease to be govermental wards, balance up the great ledger and be called men and women. Then all will be buried in the ashes of the past and our experience, having constituted one of the inevitable steps in the evolution of the human race, must necessarily grow dimmer and dimmer and eventually become so obscure as to seem altogether insignificant, as have thousands of other sanguinary epochs in the world's history."

177. The Meshwaki "Reservation" is one of the most interesting that has been visited by the writer in the East or West. Advancement is being made rapidly, but while some are buying rugs and preparing to put furnaces in their houses, others are still living in wickiups.

The present Agent (1924) is Dr. Breid, who is also Superintendent of the General Tuberculosis Hospital for Indian Children at the near by town of Toledo, where he lives. The resident executive officer is known as "The Farmer." He is the adviser and counselor of the Indians, and maintains something like a model establishment himself. There are two good schools.

A Mission House is maintained by the United Presbyterians. The work is carried forward under the direction of the Rev. R. G. Smith and his excellent wife, with most gratifying results. There is a church membership of about 45 and the good influence of the mission extends to a far larger number.

There are about 350 Indians on the "Reservation." Most of them are Meskwakis or Foxes, but there are some Saukies and a few Winnebagoes.

James Poweshiek, whose picture with his family appears in this book, is the Meskwaki policeman. His grandfather, Poweshiek, was

Chief of a band of Foxes on the site of Davenport at the time of the Black Hawk War.

The writer witnessed the building of a wickiup at a temporary Meskwaki camp at Ottumwa on the occasion of the celebration of the seventy-fifth anniversary of the founding of that city. He was surprised and delighted at the ease with which the work was done, and the firmness and apparent durability of the structure. The frame-work was made of willow poles about the size of beanpoles with the slender tops left on. The structure was to be about ten feet long. Two holes about three feet apart and with a slight inward slant were made at each end. The poles, were sharpened and jabbed down re-peatedly into these holes till they were firmly set. Then they were bent over in pairs and bound together with twine. (The inner bark of trees was doubtless used for this purpose in earlier days.) Three holes were made on each side, poles were set, drawn over to those that had already been tied together and bound to them and to each other. Two sets of poles were then bound around horizontally, and the frame was complete. The work was largely done by an old squaw with a male Indian to assist. It was interesting to see her jab the poles down into the holes with practiced hand and bind them firmly till the frame was nearly as solid as if made of two by fours.

The covering was of matting made of flags from the Iowa river, and was in rolls about four feet wide and of varying length. It was put on in overlapping layers, an apperture being left at the top, and was bound to the framework.

178. Bailey and Hair's Gazatteer, (Iowa,) pp. 257, 258, footnote. "Che-mo-ko-man" is the Saukie word for good white man.

179. John C. Sullivan was engaged in 1816 to locate the northern boundry of the Osage Indian land cession in the Territory of Mis-souri. He was the first surveyor in this part of the public domain, and he ran a line which thirty-four years later definitely became the Iowa-Missouri boundary.—*Jacob Van der Zee* in Iowa Journal of History and Politics, Vol. XIV, No. 4, p. 482.

180. Records of life upon the Half-Breed Tract are very meagre, but—they constitute the history of the first permanent settlement in Iowa. Ibid., p. 482.

181. While Black Hawk's story of this matter is rambling and disjointed, and gives his side without being modified and toned down by the other, we may safely challenge a contradiction of any of his material statements. That there are inaccuracies in it is true, but a misstatement of any material matter cannot be found. Truth with him was a cardinal virtue, and no man can truthfully say that Black

Hawk was a liar, although he withheld some facts that were essential.—*Armstrong.*

182. It is to be regretted that there is no other book in existence with this peculiar ethnic quality, nor can there be another. It would be most entertaining and instructive to study this subject from other standpoints of Indian experience and temperament, but the last Indian unmodified by the white man's schools, permanent and convenient markets, close contact, and other strong influences of civilization, has passed away.—*Rishell.*

183. Black Hawk states in his autobiography that when he was in the east his opinion was asked for on different subjects, and that he considered it his duty, after making many inquiries, to lay the most important before the public.

184. Black Hawk naively adds: "If the free states did not want them all for servants, we could take the balance in our nation to help our women make corn."

185. LeClaire was seated on the veranda of his new house, built on the treaty site. Access was by a stairway which led up from the ground and opened on the floor of the veranda at about its center.

186. This incident, narrated by George W. Logan, occured near Quenimo, Kansas in June, 1864.

187. Probably no Indian ever lived who has so caught the popular imagination as has Black Hawk. As noted elsewhere, the colossal Indian statue at Oregon, intended by the sculptor to symbolize the race, is generally referred to as "The Black Hawk Statue," and sometimes as "The Black Hawk Monument." Articles of furniture, hotels, highways and even a Division of the American Forces in the world war have been named for him. However much or little may be known about him by individuals as the years go by, his name and fame as a great Indian will be secure in a general way with the public at large.

188. As an orator his reputation extended all over the United States, among red men and white, while his good sense, liberal views and innate worth were such as to command the respect of everybody who came in contact with him, and he could be relied upon on all occasions to uphold the right. . . . Frequently was he called upon to express his views before the committees of Congress upon Indian affairs, and so great had become his reputation as an orator, that when it was known that he was to speak before these committees or the Commissioner of Indian Affairs, the grave Judges of the Supreme Court of the Unite States, together with the heads of the departments and foreign ministers, would go to hear him. This

too, although he did not speak a word of English, and his speaches had to be interpreted; but his intonation of voice, fine figurative thoughts and finished gestures were absolutely entrancing. . . .Nature made him an orator, while practice perfected what nature began, hence he was one of the very ablest speakers of his time white or red.—*Armstrong.*